**Stories from the Anne Grimes Collection
of American Folk Music**

Stories from the Anne Grimes Collection of American Folk Music

Anne Grimes

Compiled and edited by
Sara Grimes, Jennifer Grimes Kay,
Mary Grimes, and Mindy Grimes

OHIO UNIVERSITY PRESS

ATHENS

Ohio University Press, Athens, Ohio 45701
www.ohioswallow.com
© 2010 by Ohio University Press
All rights reserved

To obtain permission to quote, reprint, or
otherwise reproduce or distribute material
from Ohio University Press publications,
please contact our rights and permissions department
at (740) 593–1154 or (740) 593–4536 (fax).

Printed in the United States of America
Ohio University Press books are printed on acid-free paper ∞ ™

18 17 16 15 14 13 12 11 10   5 4 3 2 1

All photographs by James W. Grimes
are courtesy of the Grimes family.

Library of Congress Cataloging-in-Publication Data

Grimes, Anne, 1912–2004.
  Stories from the Anne Grimes collection of American folk music /
Anne Grimes ; compiled and edited by Sara Grimes ... [et al.].
    p. cm.
  Includes bibliographical references and index.
  ISBN 978-0-8214-1908-3 (hc : alk. paper) — ISBN 978-0-8214-1943-4 (pb : alk. paper)
  — ISBN 978-0-8214-4327-9 (electronic)
  1. Folk music—United States—History and criticism. 2. Folk songs—United States—Texts. 3.
Folk singers—United States—Anecdotes. I. Grimes, Sara. II. Title.
  ML3551.G77 2010
  781.62'13—dc22
                  2009049605

*(front cover photographs) Anne Grimes in Columbus, Ohio, ca. 1957.
Photo by Mac Shaffer courtesy of the* Columbus Dispatch. *Photo insets of
contributors (left to right): Arthur D. Tyler by Mac Shaffer/Columbus Dispatch;
Margaret O. Moody by James W. Grimes; Ken Ward by James W. Grimes;
Ella Strawser Flack by James W. Grimes; Brodie Franklin Halley courtesy
of Michael D. Halley; Faye Wemmer by James W. Grimes; Reuben Allen
courtesy of Gertrude R. Green*

*(photograph on page vi) Anne Grimes playing the Middletown dulcimer.
Photographer unknown*

*(back cover/flap photograph) Anne Grimes in Oberlin, Ohio, 1997.
Photo by Kimberly Barth courtesy of the* Elyria Chronicle Telegram

*(dust jacket back cover photographs) Anne Grimes holding the Middletown
dulcimer in her home in Upper Arlington, Ohio, mid-1950s. Photo by Mac Shaffer
courtesy of the* Columbus Dispatch. *Smithsonian Institution Collections,
National Museum of American History, Behring Center.*

Contents

Illustrations

Foreword

A Personal Tribute to Anne Grimes

IN THE FALL of 1956 I was beginning my senior year at Oberlin College in Ohio with a BA in physics and an unofficial "minor" in extracurricular activities, especially folk music. I fancied myself a folksinger and was immersed in the burgeoning folk scene on campus. We sponsored Pete Seeger concerts and organized a folksong club and festival. I had a radio show on WOBC and sold folk music LPs on campus. Eight of us organized a group called The Folksmiths, which toured summer camps in the northeast in 1957 and made an LP for Folkways Records. Through one of our group, David Sweet, I first met Anne Grimes in November 1956 at a weekend gathering in Chesterland, Ohio, where folksingers and collectors gathered for singing, dancing, and storytelling.

I was immediately smitten by Anne. Here was a beautiful, vibrant performer, a dulcimer and folk music collector and researcher, and the president of the Ohio Folklore Society, who seemed to know everyone in the field, including the aspiring folksinger Bob Gibson. When I asked her about possible graduate programs in folk music, she directed me to her good friend Rae (Mrs. George) Korson, head of the Archive of Folk Song at the Library of Congress (LC/FOLK), for further information. Rae in turn directed me to Indiana University, where I was soon enrolled in the MA and PhD programs in folklore and ethnomusicology. From IU a carload of us would drive each spring to the Columbus, Ohio, home of Anne and Jim Grimes and the annual meetings of the Ohio Folklore Society, where it became further evident that Anne was indeed a prime focus and conduit for the collecting, performing, and researching of folk music in the state. And for breakfast at their home, Anne would perform for us such earthy gems from her collection as "The Sea Crab."

As I began visiting LC/FOLK in 1958 and then working there in 1963, I became increasingly aware of Anne's deep association with the archive and with its director, Rae Korson, starting at least as early as February 1954, when she first visited the archive, and resulting in the duplication of her principal recordings in 1957 and 1958. Anne also served as a regional archivist for the National Federation of Music Clubs and received honorable mention for the Jo Stafford Fellowship of the American Folklore Society. After I became head of LC/FOLK in 1974, I arranged for her collection of recordings, manuscripts, and photographs to find a permanent home at the Library of

Congress. I also encouraged her to donate her important collection of dulcimers and other folk instruments to the Smithsonian Institution. I was privileged to participate in a gala event in Anne's honor at the Smithsonian in 1997. I commented then that Anne's vast collections had brought about an important cooperative effort between the national museum and the national library of the United States, her instruments and related materials residing at the Smithsonian Institution, and her recordings and over a thousand pages of manuscripts and photographs becoming a part of the Library of Congress Archive of Folk Culture. And when she eventually retired to the Kendal community in Oberlin, Ohio, what a delight it was to be able to spend time with her during my occasional visits to my alma mater, Oberlin College, where she continued to be a resource. Thank you, Anne, for your wonderful friendship and exemplary accomplishments over all those years and beyond!

Joe Hickerson
Head Emeritus
Archive of Folk Culture
American Folklife Center
Library of Congress

Preface

HAVING SPENT A long career performing, researching, and archiving the traditional music that she collected—mostly in Ohio—Anne Grimes in 2003 decided it was time to write a book featuring her favorite songs, singers, and dulcimer players.

The plan was for her writing to be accompanied by an audio CD of original performances selected from her tape-recorded collection. Featured too would be the photographs of contributors taken by her husband, James W. Grimes, who often went with her on her song- and dulcimer-collecting forays. Having selected which contributors she wanted to include, she had completed several chapters at the time of her death in January 2004, a few months before her ninety-second birthday.

In the spring of 2004, we—her daughters—decided we would finish the book for her. We were able to do this, and mostly in the words of Anne Grimes herself, thanks to our access to her extensive research, as well as to our familiarity with it. Each of us in various ways had been helping her all along. Besides, with our brother, Steve, we had grown up with the music and also were privileged to know several of her major contributors, most notably Dolly Church, Faye Wemmer, and A. B. Graham.

Especially important to Anne Grimes—and later to us—were her "contributor files." In manila folders identified by the names of each of her contributors, they are chock-full of research notes, correspondence, newspaper clippings, and transcriptions. These files were precious to her. For as long as we can remember, she kept them near her in cabinets by her desk.

We also had access to photographs; audio- and videotapes; material that she wrote, both published and unpublished; other correspondence; and her library of music books, including her notations in the books. Occasionally, we consulted outside sources, usually for verification of material referenced by her. We also visited the American Folklife Center at the Library of Congress and the Smithsonian Institution, both in Washington, D.C., to review materials she earlier had sent to them along with her tapes and dulcimers.

The songs featured in this book are her selections, and ours, from among some one thousand taped items at the American Folklife Center. The dulcimers and other instruments featured are among the forty-two instruments collected by Anne Grimes, now a part of the National Museum of American History at the Smithsonian. Both of the collections include research notes, correspondence, and other written, graphic, and taped information. Duplicates of the collection tapes are archived at the Ohio Historical Society in Columbus, Ohio.

In the 1990s Anne Grimes was recognized by Ohio State University and Ohio Wesleyan University for her lifelong accomplishments in preserving the cultural heritage of Ohio through song. At that time she thanked many people, especially her family and those mentors with whom she worked in the early days of the Ohio Folklore Society. They are included in the acknowledgments along with the many people we as editors also would like to thank for their inspiration and assistance.

Sara Grimes
Jennifer Grimes Kay
Mary Grimes
Mindy Grimes

Introduction

ANNE GRIMES HAD a gift for collecting songs—partly because she knew how and where to find them.

"Everybody thinks you find folk music in the hills; you don't . . . it's in people's heads," she told a reporter for the *Columbus Citizen-Journal* in 1971 before performing at Governor John Gilligan's Inaugural Gala at the Ohio Theater in Columbus, Ohio. Born into a pioneer Ohio family in which music had been important over the generations, Anne Grimes felt a kinship with the traditional singers she discovered. As she told the reporter: "In the folk music field, the technical term is 'informants'; I prefer to think of the people as contributors."

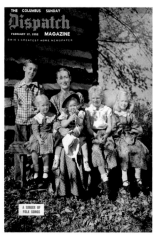

The cover of the Columbus Dispatch Sunday Magazine, *February 17, 1952: Anne Grimes with her five children—Mindy (2), Mary (4), Jennifer (6), Sara (10), and Steve (12)—in front of the Jonathan Alder cabin west of Columbus. Photo by Dan F. Prugh courtesy of the* Columbus Dispatch

During the height of her collecting and performing career in the 1950s and early 1960s, Anne Grimes sang several times at the annual National Folk Festival and recorded on Folkways. She also became an expert in the lore and techniques of the plucked or lap dulcimer (also referred to as the mountain or Appalachian dulcimer), and the Anne Grimes collection of these rare folk instruments—now housed at the Smithsonian Institution—ranks among the nation's finest. But much of her time and energy was devoted to collecting hundreds of songs and ballads that she then performed in concert-lectures with the general theme of Ohio history through song. She collected in the major cities of Columbus, Cleveland, and Cincinnati as well as in most of Ohio's eighty-eight counties, including inland cities such as Chillicothe, Greenville, Athens, Springfield, Cambridge, Lima, and Hillsboro and Ohio River Valley towns such as Gallipolis, Marietta, Steubenville, and Portsmouth.

Her "finds" included rare Child ballads (as they are known from their classifying scholar, Francis James Child) and other British survivals that she came to regard as her specialties—those songs

The map shows Ohio counties with the following names placed in their native counties:

- Williams
- Fulton
- Lucas
- Ottawa
- Lake
- Ashtabula
- Defiance
- Henry
- Wood
- Sandusky
- Erie
- Lorain
- Cuyahoga
- Geauga
- Trumbull
- Paulding / *Bodiker*
- Putnam
- Hancock
- Seneca
- Huron / *Beattie / Laylin, C.*
- Medina
- Summit
- Portage
- Mahoning
- Van Wert
- Allen
- Hardin
- Wyandot
- Crawford
- Richland / *Laylin, F.*
- Ashland
- Wayne
- Stark
- Columbiana
- Mercer
- Auglaize
- Logan
- Marion
- Morrow
- Knox
- Holmes
- Tuscarawas / *"John Funston"*
- Carroll
- Jefferson
- Shelby
- Union
- Delaware
- Coshocton
- Harrison
- Darke / *Leas*
- Champaign / *Graham*
- Miami / *Wilson*
- Clark
- Franklin / *Tyler*
- Licking / *Beecher / Langstaff / Utter*
- Muskingum / *Allen, R.*
- Guernsey
- Belmont / *Bacon*
- Preble
- Montgomery / *Cox*
- Greene
- Madison
- Fayette
- Pickaway
- Fairfield
- Perry
- Morgan
- Noble
- Monroe
- Butler
- Warren
- Clinton
- Ross / *Flack / Weinrich / Moody*
- Hocking
- Vinton / *White, Bob*
- Athens
- Washington
- Hamilton
- Highland
- Pike
- Jackson / *Harper / McNerlin*
- Meigs / *Church / Wood*
- *White, Anne / White, Bird / Randolph*
- Clermont
- Brown
- Adams
- Scioto / *Reno / Rickey*
- Gallia
- *Allen, F. / Halley / Ward / Swick / Ralston*
- *Hook / Wemmer*
- Lawrence / *Fullen / Lunsford, W. / Fields*
- Ohio River
- Lake Erie

(above) Some significant names related to the Anne Grimes Collection, placed in their native counties. Map source: Ohio Department of Natural Resources

related to or patterned after old English, Irish, or Scottish ballads and folksongs. As she wrote in her liner notes to her Folkways record: "These are recognizable by their antique tunes, or 'airs,' often almost chant-like, in minor keys, or gapped-scale modes. The impersonal ballad stories are often sung in 'old style,' with straightforward, clear diction, odd melodic ornamentations, and unexpected held notes and rhythm shifts."

The bawdy songs Anne Grimes collected she considered some of the most important and choice of her early material. She rarely performed her bawdy ballads—and then only the mildly bawdy ones such as Bessie Weinrich's "Big Shirt"—but she appreciated them on many levels and researched them to their Renaissance and even medieval roots.

As for the homegrown Ohio songs, contributors sang songs about wars in the Ohio territory, transportation, political campaigns, the temperance movement, American Indians, and the Underground Railroad. The Anne Grimes Collection also includes songs about everyday life; local ballads about murders, train wrecks, and scandals; as well as hymns, minstrel material, children's songs, and popular composed songs such as those of Dan Emmett and Benjamin Hanby.

A proud Buckeye herself, Anne Grimes asserted that Ohioans generally are proud, if not sentimental, about their state's complex and diverse history as represented in these songs. In her liner notes to her Folkways record, she wrote:

> They boast of Edison (Light) and the Wright Brothers (Flight) and tell of renowned Buckeye educators, statesmen, authors, composers, entertainers and reformers; and of agricultural, religious and industrial leaders, and, of course, the eight "Ohio Presidents."
>
> The state's area, between the "Great River" (the Ohio) and Lake Erie, has geographical advantages, natural resources and beauty, which have made it a center of transportation and trade since prehistoric times. It drew French trappers and explorers to the "Beautiful River," made the "Ohio Country" a contested battleground before and after the Revolution, and caused "Ohio Fever" to inspire its pioneer settlement....
>
> Ohio is also proud of its place as a median or average cross-section of the country. Even the vegetation is a combination of southern Appalachians, Great Plains and Lake. Ohioans speak with unregional accent, sounding "southern" to New Englanders and "northern" to natives of the "Deep South," although phrases, terms and inflections from both are recognizable, especially as surviving in the regions of the early land grants.
>
> Many of the descendants of Ohio's first settlers live on their families' original land grants. During the period of the westward movement, Buckeyes profited by the many emigrants who passed through the area by the National Road, the canals, rivers and lakes, and, by so doing, became better established and more firmly rooted in the state.

Anne Laylin Grimes was born in Columbus, Ohio, in 1912. Among her earliest memories was the singing of family songs by her parents, Clarence D. and Fanny Hagerman Laylin, and by her grandparents and other relatives. Musical evenings sometimes involved chamber music with her father on cello; her brother, Ned, and sister, Louise, on violins; and her mother and Anne herself on the A. B. Chase grand piano. Her schooling in music began at the age of five with piano study, and she continued to study piano, music theory, and voice through high school and college. Following her graduation with both Bachelor of Arts and Bachelor of Music degrees from Ohio Wesleyan University in 1934, she completed course credits for a master's degree in music history at Ohio State University, where she was a soloist with the Ohio State University Concert Choir.

Anne Grimes tape-recording Mrs. J. W. Haigler in her Washington Court House, Ohio, home, contributing to the Anne Grimes Collection, mid-1950s. Photo by James W. Grimes

A classically trained musician and accomplished pianist, Anne Grimes from 1942 to 1946 served as music and dance critic for the *Columbus Citizen* newspaper in Columbus, Ohio. Earlier, from 1940 to 1942, she hosted a music series on WOSU radio for which she was arranger, writer of program notes, and accompanist, as well as piano and vocal soloist. One week, when a planned program collaborator became ill just before broadcast time and she had to carry on alone, she played and sang some of her grandmother's songs. Favorable listener reaction included contributions of similar passed-down family and community songs, marking the beginning of her folk music collection.

At first, she captured songs on paper through musical notation. In 1953, however, she was able to begin recording sound on magnetic tape, thanks to her purchase of a state-of-the-art Magnecorder, a reel-to-reel tape recorder with fine fidelity. During the 1950s alone, she tape-recorded some 170 people. She often collected on her own, sometimes daring winter storms, floods, and other barriers as she took off in the family station wagon in search of traditional music, her only companion her Magnecorder, which weighed some fifty pounds. But often she was accompanied by her husband, Dr.

James W. Grimes helps restore the oil painting Perry's Victory *by William Powell (1865), on display in the Rotunda of the Ohio Statehouse in Columbus, 1946.* Columbus Citizen, *Scripps-Howard Newspapers/Grandview Heights Public Library/Photohio.org*

Anne Grimes with her children, Jennifer, Mary, Sara, Steve, and Mindy, 1951. Photo by Dan F. Prugh courtesy of the Columbus Dispatch

Following a performance in Lima, Ohio, in May 1953, Anne Grimes listens to a member of the audience, Mrs. Frances Kelley, share her knowledge of both local history and songs. Photo by Robert K. Waldron courtesy of the Lima News

James W. Grimes, and sometimes by one or more of their five children.

A graduate of Cornell University in landscape architecture with a PhD in fine arts from Ohio State University, James Grimes, who died in 1981, was a professor in the Department of Fine Arts at Ohio State from 1934 to 1961 and chairman of the Department of Art at Denison University from 1961 to 1970. He also was a professional artist: a painter/craftsman, portraitist, and art historian. His work included the extensive collecting, restoring, preserving, publishing, and exhibiting of Ohio art for the Ohio Historical Society. Born in 1902 into a Cambridge, Ohio, family descended from Guernsey County pioneers, he understood and supported Anne Grimes's work harvesting and saving a generally overlooked musical heritage of Ohio and the Midwest.

Sharing his wife's excitement over her growing collection of folksongs and dulcimers, James Grimes helped her in many ways, including designing the costumes she wore in performance, accompanying her on collecting trips, and locating dulcimers. His enjoyment of the people and places they visited together on her collecting trips is evident in the photographs he took. Works of art themselves, and featured throughout this book, these photographs became an important part of the documentation of the Anne Grimes collections.

As for the Grimes children, we were often the first to hear our mother's version of a newly collected song as she practiced her singing on us before performing in public: "If I hear the kids humming the tune of a song around the house, I know it's a good one," she said. To help illustrate in her lecture/recitals how folksongs change as they are handed down, she noted our adaptation of "Aunt Rhodie," in which we had the goose dying in the mailbox rather than in the millpond. As she explained, millponds "aren't very real to city children."

Contributors to the Anne Grimes Collection included many fine singers with sureness of rhythm, pitch, and melody, although few had

Margaret O. Moody with Anne Grimes in Chillicothe, Ohio, 1955. Photo by James W. Grimes

any formal musical training. Rating her singers as "uniquely good," she added that this may well have stemmed from the prevalence of singing schools in Ohio, lasting through the nineteenth century.

In an interview in 1980 with Dr. Ellen Gibb, a folk scholar who was then at Ohio State University, Anne Grimes said of her contributors:

> From the very aristocratic to just the country guys or some of the lovely old ladies—I always knew when I had a real contributor. And the funny part about it, there's one or two that I just got one song from that had been "their" song for years. But there again, it was something that was very special.

Most contributors were from families that had lived in Ohio for several generations, and they were representative of the complexity and diversity of Buckeye tradition. They were homemakers, poets, farmers, educators, businesspeople, lawyers, ministers, artists, domestic workers, and politicians. Some were members of her own family, chief among them her mother, who was from a Richland County, Ohio, pioneer family. Some Anne Grimes met only once. Others became close friends who visited often in her home, as she did in theirs. Some she invited to perform with her and, with her encouragement, some of her major contributors participated in Ohio Folklore Society meetings during the 1950s, when she served as secretary-treasurer, editor of the newsletter, and president.

Anne Grimes in her Granville, Ohio, home, early 1960s.
Photo courtesy of the Columbus Dispatch

Contributors also attended "great and productive" singing gatherings at the Grimes home in Columbus, where they traded songs and stories among themselves and with other invited guests. Major contributors such as John Bodiker, Sarah Basham, Bertha Bacon, Arthur Tyler, Faye Wemmer, and William Lunsford joined in the singing at parties that also might include folk experts and scholars such as Dr. Francis Utley, the Ohio State English professor who helped found the Ohio Folklore Society. Several of these musical gatherings in the Grimes household were tape-recorded to become part of the Anne Grimes Collection, most notably the party she gave for guest of honor Carl Sandburg, the author, poet, and folklorist.

Most of the traditional singers in the Anne Grimes Collection sang unaccompanied, though a few played guitar or banjo. Her introduction to the dulcimer came in 1952 when she saw one in a craft shop in Asheville, North Carolina, where she participated in Bascom Lamar Lunsford's Mountain Dance and Folk Festival. She was able to find the maker, Wade Martin, a baseball player who whittled in the off-season and who came from a family of fiddle makers, including his father, Marcus Martin. She took the Wade Martin dulcimer home, "fiddled with it," tried to learn what she could about dulcimer history, and began to create dulcimer arrangements for her songs.

As she began taking along her dulcimer to lecture-recitals, the instrument attracted the attention of people in the audience who had seen one or had one at home. That was the beginning—using the Wade Martin dulcimer as "bait"—of her discovery of a living tradition of dulcimer players in central and southern Ohio. This discovery

Anne Grimes holding the Middletown dulcimer in her home in Upper Arlington, Ohio, mid-1950s.
Photo by Mac Shaffer courtesy of the Columbus Dispatch. *Smithsonian Institution Collections,*
National Museum of American History, Behring Center

of dulcimers north of the Ohio River was a surprise to folk scholars, and to her. Her tape-recordings of Ohio players—represented in this book by Brodie Halley, W. E. Lunsford, Jane Jones McNerlin, Arthur Tyler, Lilly McGhee Ward Swick, Ken Ward, Bob White, and Okey Wood—include their discussions about dulcimer technique and lore.

Meanwhile, she also began collecting dulcimers, ending up with thirty-one pre-1940 vintage dulcimers that include eleven from Ohio and the rest from Kentucky, West Virginia, Virginia, Pennsylvania, and Tennessee. Most are from the Upper Ohio River Valley area, where she came to believe the dulcimer originated, although she agreed with the majority of scholars that the origins of this native American instrument remain obscure.

By 1955, her preferred performance instrument was an old walnut dulcimer she found in Middletown, Hamilton County, Ohio, that she especially liked for its wide fretboard and rich tone. She explained that, like violins, dulcimers get better as they age. She replaced the Middletown dulcimer's original horizontal hand-forged iron tuning pins with cello pegs and played it almost exclusively until 1966, when she commissioned Ohio dulcimer maker Ron Chacey to make a more durable copy. From then on, she played the Chacey dulcimer, also a fine dulcimer. How to tell a good one? Anne Grimes said: "You can heft one and tell if it is good. It's light, with a solidity in the middle."

As a folksinger and dulcimer player, Anne Grimes followed the traditional styles she learned from contributors. Her playing and singing can be heard on her 1957 Folkways record *Ohio State Ballads: History through Folk Songs: Anne Grimes, with Dulcimer,* which has been reissued on both tape and CD by Smithsonian Folkways Recordings. Most of her live performances were at local venues, for folklore society groups, music organizations, folk festival audiences, historical meetings, and state and regional civic, cultural, political, agricultural, and religious groups. She always hoped that her performances of songs she had collected would elicit still more songs from her audiences. Attired in costumes patterned after dresses worn by her own great-grandmother in Ohio one hundred years before, she nearly always asked: "Does my singing remind you of any songs from your own family?" And people often responded by approaching her after a performance with the invitation: "Come see us—my mother sings."

This singing with the hope of inspiring others to sing, whether on stage or in individual sessions with contributors, Anne Grimes called "priming the pump" of the well of memory. In performance, she helped the process by gearing her programs to the locale of the venues she played. In Mt. Vernon, Ohio, for instance, she might sing "Old Dan Tucker," attributed to Mt. Vernon native Dan Emmett; in Portsmouth, Ohio, she might include a canal song or two.

Anne Grimes in Columbus, Ohio, ca. 1957. Photo by Mac Shaffer courtesy of the Columbus Dispatch

In a December 1954 column in the *Columbus Citizen* on one of her performances in Columbus, Ben Hayes caught the Anne Grimes style:

> Girl singers are all the time sitting on grand pianos—you've seen them. Well, Anne Grimes, Ohio's famous searcher-outer of folk songs, climbed right to the top of an upright piano, without any assistance, this week at Schiller Park, an autoharp in one hand, a dulcimer in the other—making, let us say, a noteworthy impression on members of the Columbus Grandmothers Club.
>
> And then she sang. In that Grimes golden voice, Anne sang the warning songs and the answering-back songs the grandmothers of the grandmothers once had sung to them.
>
> She projected the old songs with verve, picking the dulcimer on her calico lap with a turkey feather, while perched half-way up the wall—hers was a hi-fi performance.
>
> And spicy, too. One leg-o'mutton sleeve slid from an attractive shoulder; Anne's petticoat flashed white as she tapped her foot to her spirited singing of Old Dan Tucker. That followed:
> "Whistling girls and crowing hens
> Always come to no good end."

"I am priming the pump," Anne told the grandmothers. "I want you to remember the songs your grandmothers sang as they worked—as they kneaded bread, as they fried chicken, and the songs they sang to lull you to sleep. It just isn't done today—I guess TV has replaced the old songs."

She began with "Ohio fever" tunes, which includes "The Little Mohee" and "Come Along, Young Lovers," and ran through several pump-priming categories, mentioning the sad ballads, the murder songs, and even Red Skelton's favorite, which urges someone to go and tell Aunt Rhodie that the old gray goose is drowned in the mill pond.

She produced results. Eyes lighted up, heads nodded, feet were tapping to the old Dan Tucker rhythm. . . .

Meanwhile, in the Ohio countryside, Ruth S. Morgan, a columnist for the *Quaker City Home Towner,* described the spirit of Anne Grimes's singing and collecting when she was booked as a main evening attraction at the 1958 Hill Town Folk Festival during the annual homecoming at Senecaville in Guernsey County:

Home Coming festivities are once more history and our town has again settled back into its usual calm. With the exception of the children, perhaps no one enjoyed the affair more than Mrs. Anne Grimes, of Columbus, one of the program attractions arranged by officials for the celebration. Mrs. Grimes represented the Hill Folk Festival portion of the program, she being a noted Ohio folksong singer and balladeer. With her pleasing personality (and in old-fashioned dress) she charmed the people who came to the Open House, held for her on Friday afternoon at Garfield Hall, with her singing and playing and general sociability.

Ohio Hills Folk Festival poster designed and printed by Frank A. Morgan. Reproduced with permission of Terry F. Morgan. Smithsonian Institution Collections, National Museum of American History, Behring Center

Her dulcimer, an old-fashioned stringed instrument of pioneer days, was a musical instrument of interest and one with which many folks were not familiar and in some cases had never before seen. She explained the methods of playing it and sang many tunes for the guests, at intervals between the serving of punch and cookies.

Quite interested in hearing old songs and tunes—the "handed down" kind coming from parents and grandparents

Anne Grimes at home in Granville, Ohio, 1987. Photo by Julie Elman

that linger in one's mind—she prevailed upon Mrs. Laura Carpenter, local resident but formerly of Monroe County, to sing and tape record one called "The True Maiden" for her. . . .

Mrs. Grimes didn't stop with the Open House hours, however, as immediately following she went to call on Mrs. Laura (Hartley) Lingo, one of the community's oldest residents, who is much interested in music but was unable to get to the hall.

She later visited with Mrs. Daisy (Arnold) Wilcox. . . . She mingled and talked with folks at the Methodist church where she ate her supper, and her scheduled appearance on the platform at the Home Coming grounds that evening drew a large number of listeners. Following the program, she sloshed up through the soggy grounds and stopped and chatted with the Apple Butter stirrers, and then to our house for coffee and cookies, and here the apparently indefatigable folksong expert announced she was coming back in the morning to visit Salesville.

Her Friday night appearance ended her official visit here, but she had not yet had enough and after spending the night with friends at Senecaville, she came back on Saturday. In the morning she called on Mrs. Winnie Reynolds at Salesville, the lady in charge of the Apple Butter stirrin' the night before, seeking old tunes, information on Morgan's Raiders and other historical facts. She and Mrs. Reynolds joined in singing an old war song, "Goodbye Ma, Goodbye Pa," and she made acquaintance with the Reynolds' daughter, Mrs. T.W. St. Clair, Columbus, whom she later expects to contact in regard to a book of folk songs.

Another visitor, Chas. O. Reynolds, Zanesville, furnished her with some information on the Morgan Raiders. Before she left, she purchased some of the Home Coming apple butter.

Mrs. Grimes then came on to Quaker City and viewed the Saturday parade and mingled with more people. Again she unloaded her dulcimer and favored with an impromptu "sing" on the Wilcox porch, for Mrs. Wilcox and several interested folks who congregated there. After that, she graciously showed her instrument and sang a tune or two for workers at the church lunch stand who had been unable to get away to hear her on Friday.

Mrs. Grimes was pleased with her visit here and was interested in people in this locality. It has been suggested that she should visit Calais people over in Monroe County who could, no doubt, give her some old ballads and folk tunes. She has many in her collection and this is one I like for its vibrant ring:

A, B, C, D, E, F, G,
H, I, J, K, L-M,
N, O, P, Q, R, S, T,
And that's the way to spell 'em.
Then comes U and then comes V;
Let the chorus ring 'em,
W, and X, Y, Z,
And that's the way to sing 'em.

Anne Grimes conducted her "hunting trips" and research related to her developing collection of Ohio folk music largely independent of any public or institutional aid. When she started her folklore work in the 1940s and early 1950s, academe in Ohio offered little in folklore studies. Recognized folklore scholars did offer courses in individual disciplines like sociology, music, anthropology, and linguistics at nearby Indiana University and the University of Pennsylvania, with less extensive offerings at Detroit's Wayne State, and in Kentucky and West Virginia. But scholars in these institutions were unaware of the extent of a surviving "live" Buckeye folk music tradition before her discoveries.

That is not to say that she worked in isolation. She had support from many other folk performers, scholars, and collectors. Her tape collection, for instance, includes songs shared with her by Bob Gibson, the folksinger; Bascom Lamar Lunsford, the folklore expert;

as well as her fellow performers at the National Folk Festival in St. Louis: May Kennedy McCord, Pete Seeger, and Jenny Wells Vincent. Besides the Ohio Folklore Society, organizations helpful to her included the Ohio Historical Society, which cited her in 1958 for "distinctive contributions to the history of the State of Ohio." But more formal recognition for her work came only much later, when she was awarded in 1993 the Ohio State University School of Music Distinguished Career in Music Award and in 1994 the Ohio Wesleyan University Alumni Association's Distinguished Achievement Citation.

Anne Grimes wanted to prove to scholars that there was traditional music worth saving in Ohio, and she delighted in sharing her discoveries with them. Her greatest satisfaction, however, came in demonstrating to the contributors themselves—as well as to their families and even their communities—the value of their songs. As she told the reporter for the *Columbus Citizen-Journal* in 1971:

> Someone will invariably say after a performance, "Why, I just remembered a song my grandmother or grandfather or Uncle Harry used to sing you might like. . . ." Sometimes I already know the source of it, quite often I don't. . . . So I look and ask for all the historical help I can get.
>
> It's a wonderful feeling to help people sort of "find" something that's really belonged to them all along.

As a traditional performer with strong Ohio roots, Anne Grimes thought she had an advantage—in contrast to what she called "itinerant" professional folklorists—in harvesting and saving an overlooked musical heritage in her home state. With forebearers on both sides who were active in the state's development, she credited this background with giving her invaluable local contacts; knowledge of local history, sentiments, and opinions; and historical information and facts behind the local material she collected. In her liner notes to her Folkways record, she explained:

> I have found that my contributors' previous unawareness that their "old songs" were folksongs has been an advantage in collection, since their singing has an unspoiled spontaneity and authenticity, possibly not available today where traditional singers have become more self-conscious or fit their renditions to preconceived "folk" molds.

Most of the tape-recorded material in the Anne Grimes Collection, collected from 1953 to 1957, was duplicated by the Library of Congress in 1958. The Grimes family moved in 1962 from Upper Arlington, a suburb of Columbus, to the village of Granville, Ohio. Anne Grimes lived in Granville for the next thirty-three years, in a historic 1834 house across the street from Denison University. As time and health permitted, she continued to give programs throughout Ohio and the Midwest. She also served as a judge from the early

1960s to 1992 at Dulcimer Days at Roscoe Village, Ohio, a festival she helped found, as well as at a number of other national and regional festivals.

Anne Grimes did some collecting of songs and lore in the Granville area, but increasingly she turned her attention to organizing and sharing her audiotape and dulcimer collections. She archived her research notes, transcriptions, letters, and other materials, partly with the help of two assistants made possible by a grant from the Ohio Arts Council in 1978. As she became known to new generations of folklorists, she welcomed visitors from around the country to her home, including scholars, folksingers, and dulcimer makers and players who came and stayed, sometimes for days.

During the 1980s, Anne Grimes worked with the Ohio Historical Society on duplicating her original tape recordings. Also during the 1980s, several audio- and videotapes about the Anne Grimes collections of folksongs and dulcimers were made at the Grimes home in Granville, including more than fourteen hours of audiotape interviews conducted by Dr. Ellen Gibb, the folk scholar who was then at Ohio State University; an audiotape interview with Anne Grimes conducted by Penelope Niven McJunkin for the Carl Sandburg Oral History Project; and a presentation by Anne Grimes of her dulcimer collection videotaped by Harold Heckendorn, retired sound engineer and volunteer for the Ohio Historical Society.

In 1995 Anne Grimes moved to Kendal at Oberlin, a Quaker-affiliated retirement community in Oberlin, Ohio, where she occasionally continued to collect songs and give programs. Her last performance on a national stage was at the Smithsonian Institution in 1997. There she talked about her dulcimers, showed slides of some of her favorite contributors, played her dulcimer, and sang along with her old friend Joe Hickerson, then head of the Archive of Folk Culture at the Library of Congress.

Traveling along the highways and byways of Ohio in the 1950s as a folksinger and collector of traditional music, Anne Grimes encountered a host of people who opened up their homes to her to share their most precious family heirlooms—their songs. She tape-recorded these treasures for posterity and further preserved them through her lecture-recitals all over Ohio—from the state capital of Columbus to lake towns in the north and river towns in the south—and beyond. In performance, she never failed to acknowledge the source of her material—her contributors. In this book, Anne Grimes shares with a new audience both the music and her stories about the people who sang, played, and otherwise contributed to preserving our musical heritage.

Anne Grimes in Granville, Ohio, mid-1980s. Photo by Barbara Vogel reproduced with permission

Frank Allen with the author in Rio Grande, Ohio, early 1950s. Photos by James W. Grimes. Anne Grimes Collection, American Folklife Center, Library of Congress

Scantling collected by the author in Viper, Kentucky. Photo by David A. Kay

1 Frank Allen

Scantlings and the Singleton Dulcimer

GALLIA
COUNTY

DULCIMERS ARE RARELY ever just alike—even those made by the same maker. They vary with available woods, with how handy the maker is with a penknife, or with what other dulcimers the maker has seen. Since Biblical times, many different instruments have been called "dulcimers." In Ohio, I found that dulcimers go by a number of names, but never by the three-syllable "dulc-i-more" as is pronounced in the southern mountains.

Frank Allen neither owned nor played a dulcimer, but he was of great interest to my collecting of dulcimer lore. For he was my first authentic source for the name "scantling" (pronounced "scantlin'") for the large, boxy dulcimers—a term and examples of which I later found in West Virginia and Kentucky.

I'm not sure how I got onto Frank Allen and his lovely wife, Miriam, of Rio Grande (pronounced Rye-Oh Grande). This beautiful small college town in southeastern Ohio is near the farm that was owned by Bob Evans, the home-style restaurant chain originator. So the Allens, who for many years ran a grocery store and hotel in town, may have sought me out after I sang and judged at a well-attended Bob Evans Farm folk festival and competition. Unfortunately, this contact was before I tape-recorded contributors.

Frank Allen vividly remembered that when Gallia and Jackson counties were being lumbered in the late 1870s, lumbermen made rough dulcimers out of two-by-four pieces of lumber known as scantlings. In time the instruments themselves became known as scantlings. Scantlings, according to Allen, made a very loud sound and were often used at lumbermen's Saturday night dances. I later found that Native American lumbermen working in northern Michigan demanded scantlings for their Saturday night dances as a part of their pay.

My husband Jimmie and I found my scantling in Corbin, Kentucky, which is about eighty miles from Viper, Kentucky, and the home of Jean Ritchie, whose performance and writing about her singing and dulcimer tradition have been vital to research and continuation.

In the 1950s at the Berea Inn in Berea, Kentucky, I happened to meet Jean's sister, Edna Ritchie Baker. She was attending a folk festival, and my family was staying at the inn while on our way home from a visit with my mother-in-law in Asheville, North Carolina. Edna told me that Will Singleton—the Viper, Kentucky, dulcimer maker—sometimes made large box-type dulcimers. She later described such a Singleton dulcimer to L. Allen Smith for his book *A Catalogue of Pre-Revival Appalachian Dulcimers:*

> He made several dulcimers, I don't know how many, he probably made a hundred or so. The first one we had that he made was a great big long dulcimer, about that [1 m] long and it was box shaped. Just squared off on the corners and had a wonderful tone. It was in my family for a while then it got lost.

Though the maker of my scantling is unknown—and L. Allen Smith disagrees with me—I maintain that it could be a Singleton. In any case, the information from the Ritchies combined with my having found the scantling in their area helps identify the instrument as probably having been made in Kentucky.

My dulcimer collection does include an undisputed Singleton, donated to me by the New York Public Library. It had been willed to the library, which at the time had no use for it, so Maria Cimino, the library's children's room librarian (and author of books for children), suggested it be sent to me. Mrs. Cimino learned of my collection when we were friends and fellow Ohio State University faculty wives. The dulcimer has a label inside the right sound hole that reads "Viper, KY, W.C. Singleton; No. of dulcimer 83/ August 2, 1939, my age 79 years."

Frank Allen in Rio Grande, Ohio, early 1950s. Photo by James W. Grimes

Reuben Allen in Zanesville, Ohio, December 1949. Photo courtesy of Gertrude R. Green

2 Reuben Allen

The Homestead Strike • My Eyes Are Dim

MUSKINGUM COUNTY

WHEN WE MET seventy-one-year-old Reuben Allen in his hometown of Zanesville in Muskingum County, Ohio, he worked as a houseman for a prominent Zanesville family and also occasionally tended bar and entertained at a country club, where he sang and played guitar at private parties. His songs included his own compositions as well as some he learned in travels around the world after he joined the navy in 1909.

An African American whose parents came to Zanesville from Leesburg, Virginia, Reuben also sang family songs like his mother's lullaby "Who Killed Cock Robin" and murder ballads like "Charles Guiteau" and "Pearl Bryan." A skilled performer, he accompanied himself on guitar on all his songs, and he made Jimmie and me laugh with his falsetto version of "Reuben Reuben, I've Been Thinking."

I also taped Reuben's recounting of several routines from his minstrel days when, as a youth of about eighteen, he joined a traveling tent show that came to Zanesville in wagons selling patent

Reuben Allen (left) with his wife, Ada (right); their daughter Gertrude; and Gertrude's husband, Sam; Zanesville, Ohio, 1951. Photo courtesy of Gertrude R. Green

medicine. His minstrel songs included a parody of Mendelssohn's "Spring Song" (titled "Meddlesome Springtime Song"), and "My Eyes Are Dim," the popular nineteenth-century parody of the practice of lining out hymns in church, in which the minister intoned a line that was taken up in turn by the congregation.

One of the songs I liked best that Reuben Allen sang was about the Underground Railroad, the popular name for the system aiding escaped slaves from the South to reach Canada. Unfortunately, I did not get it down on tape, but I did include it on my Folkways album. The song reflects that although slavery was barred by its constitution when Ohio became a state in 1803, escaped slaves were still not safe in Ohio because of the "Fugitive Slave" and "Black" laws.

Reuben's version of "The Underground Railroad" had a different tune and fewer words than the song as composed and published in 1854 by Joshua McCarty Simpson, an African American abolitionist who attended Oberlin College. Simpson lived in Putnam, Ohio—an abolitionist settlement across the Muskingum River from Zanesville.

Another important song Reuben sang was "The Homestead Strike," a ballad-like union song that tells about a mine fire started in 1884 near New Straitsville, a town just south of Zanesville in Perry County. The fire was still burning at the time of our tape recording in 1953!

My Eyes Are Dim

(Spoken)

"Brothers and sisters, we'll take my text this morning
  from the 14th chapter of Clover."
  Then the deacon got up and says, "Brother Johnson, you don't
  mean Clover, you mean Timothy." He says, "That's it, Deacon Jones,
  that's it. I knowed it was some kind of the pasture grass." So he says,
"Now we'll sing number 18. My eyes are dim; I cannot see. I left my
  specs at home." And the choir, the church, says:

(Sung)

"My eyes are dim: I cannot see; I left my specs at home."

(Spoken)

Preacher said, "I did not mean for you to sing. I was only telling you."

(Sung)

"I did not mean for you to sing. I was only telling you."

(Spoken)

He said, "The devil is certainly in you all. That ain't no hymn at all."

(Sung)

"The devil is certainly in you all. That ain't no hymn at all."

(Spoken)

He says, "Doxology, Doxology."

The Homestead Strike

A man who fights for his honor, none can blame him.
May peace be with him wherever he will roam.
No child of his could ever go to condemn him.
A man who fights for his honor and his home.

It was a frosty morning when the fire was set.
The band was a'playing in the snow.
But nobody knows except the union leader
That what was taking place in the hole.
When they heard the boom, when they heard it boom
And the [men come running] up.

Oh, the man who fights for his honor none can blame him.
He fights for his honor and his home.

3 Bertha Bacon

Lord Lovel · The Death of the Devil · Johnny Sands

BELMONT
COUNTY

AT THE TIME I tape-recorded her in her home in 1956, Bertha Bacon was living in Columbus not far from the Ohio State University campus. She heard about me and just called me up.

Bertha Bacon remembered the songs that her mother, Lily Nace Damsel, sang to the family—including nine children—in Barnesville, Belmont County, Ohio. Like most singers of traditional songs, Mrs. Bacon sang unaccompanied, including her version of "Lord Lovel," which she called "Rosie and the Briar," after its last line.

With its unusual and interesting tune, her "Lord Lovel" was one of just three songs Mrs. Bacon contributed to my collection—but all are important and all became part of my performance repertoire. What makes "Lord Lovel" particularly important is that it is a Child ballad, one of twenty-seven versions and variants of Child ballads that I found still being sung traditionally in Ohio in the 1950s.

Child ballads are the classic British ballads that go way, way back—some from as early as the thirteenth century. They are called Child ballads after the Harvard scholar, Francis James Child, who classified and numbered the 305 ballads he researched and published in the late 1800s. Of course, contributors never announced these ballads to me as "Child." At times when I inadvertently exclaimed, "Why that's a Child ballad," they would say, "Why certainly, I learned it as a child!"

"The Death of the Devil" is obviously Irish. This rare little song may well have come to America with Mrs. Bacon's maternal ancestor, an "English lady" who eloped to Philadelphia with the family's Irish gardener. The couple eventually settled in Belmont County. Mrs. Bacon said that she sang the refrain a little differently from the way an older brother did. He started the refrain with "Whack!"

As for "Johnny Sands," Mrs. Bacon said, "This one was the one, of course, we loved the best of all."

Lord Lovel (Child #75)

Lady Nancee in her chamber so high
Lord Lovel went riding by, by, by.
Lord Lovel went riding by.

"Oh, where are you going, Lord Lovel?" she cried.
"Oh, where are you going?" cried she.
"I'm going," said he, "to some foreign country.
 Some foreign country to view, view, view,
 Some foreign country to view."

"When will you be back? When will you be back?
 When will you be back?" cried she.
"I will be back in years, two or three,
 To my fair Lady Nancee, cee, cee,
 To my fair Lady Nancee."

 He hadn't been gone three weeks and three days,
 When thoughts came into his mind,
"I must return, I must return,
 To the girl I left behind, hind, hind.
 To the girl I left behind."

 Oh, he rode and he rode and
 he rode at full speed.
 'Til he came to St. Patrick's town.
 And then he heard the church bell ringing,
 The people all gathered around, round, round,
 The people all gathered around.

"Oh, what is the matter," Lord Lovel he cried.
"Oh, what is the matter?" cried he.
"There is a woman dead in this town.
 Some called her Lady Nancee, cee, cee.
 Some called her Lady Nancee."

Oh, he begged for the coffin to be opened,
The sheets to be folded down.
And there he kissed her clay-cold lips,
And the tears came trickling down, down, down.
And the tears came trickling down.

Lady Nancee was buried in the churchyard.
Lord Lovell was buried beside her.
When up from her grave
there sprung a rose,
And up from his'n a briar, iar, iar.
And up from his'n a briar.

They grew and they grew
to the high steeple top
Till they could grow no higher.
They linked, they locked
in a true lover's knot,
The rosie and the briar, iar, iar.
The rosie and the briar.

The Death of the Devil

'Twas on a frosty night,
And I was very poor,
And, as you may suppose,
The Devil came into the door.
In his hands he held a large hook
And his eyes they sparkled bright.
Said he to my sister Sook, "Sook!
Where's your brother Mike?"

Refrain:
Sing fathery eye-re-eye.
Sing oraful-oraful, oraful, oraful, oh!

My little brother Mike,
He'd heard his voice before.
And, lively as a linnet,
He jumped behind the door.
The Devil stamped and swore,
And with sulfur filled the room,
When he saw poor little Mike
Hiding behind the broom.
Refrain

My little sister Peg,
She had a wonderful knack.
And with my father's wooden leg
She broke the Devil's back.
'Twas on a washing day
And the water was boiling hot.
She gave to him left and right
And tumbled him into the pot.
Refrain

Next day the Devil died;
'Twas joyful news to hear.
And as you may suppose
He was buried in the bottom of the sphere.
So now you've nothing to fear.
Let your glasses sparkle bright,
For since the Devil's dead,
You can do just what you like.
Refrain

Johnny Sands

There was a man named Johnny Sands.
He married Betty Hague.
And though she brought him gold and land,
She proved a terrible plague.

For oh, she was a scolding wife,
Full of caprice and whim.
He said that he was tired of life,
She said she was tired of him,
That she was tired of him.

Said he, "My love, I'll drown myself,
The river runs below."
Cried she, "Pray do, you silly elf,
I've wished it long ago."

"Now down upon the brink I'll stand,
While you run down the hill,
And push me in with all your might."
Said she, "My love, I will."
Said she, "My love, I will."

"For fear that I should courage lack
And try to save my life,
Pray tie my hands behind my back."
"I will," replied his wife.

She tied them fast, as you may think,
And when securely done,
"Now stand," she said, "Upon the brink
And I'll prepare to run,
And I'll prepare to run."

Now down the hill came his loving wife.
She ran with all her force
To push him in; he stepped aside;
And she fell in, of course.

So, splashing, dashing like a fish,
"Oh save me, Johnny Sands!"
"I cannot, my love, though much I wish,
For you have tied my hands,
For you have tied my hands!"

Bertha Basham Wright (left) and her mother, Sarah Basham, both contributed significant traditional ballads to the Anne Grimes Collection. Columbus, Ohio, 1957. Photo by Mac Shaffer courtesy of the Columbus Dispatch

4 Sarah Basham and Bertha Basham Wright

Lass of Roch Royal • Seafaring Man • It Rained a Mist

SARAH BASHAM AND HER daughter, Bertha Basham Wright, were both marvelous, old-style singers. Sometimes they sang together, each helping the other to remember the words. They had wonderful songs, including six Child ballads. Sarah Basham was eighty-two when I tape-recorded them in 1957 at their family home in Columbus.

Originally from West Virginia, Mrs. Basham knew her version of "Lass of Roch Royal" (Child #76) as "One Morning in May," from its first line. Actually this is only a fragment of the ballad, and she remembered that there had been more of it. Verses 2 and 3 of her "One Morning in May" seem to have come from "Young Hunting" (Child #68), and even Mrs. Basham admitted the similarity of her

"Lass of Roch Royal" as sung by Sarah Basham. Notation by the author

tune to that of her "House Carpenter" (Child #243) which she also contributed in a full, thirteen-versed version.

This very mixture is typical of what sometimes happens after generations of passing down a ballad orally: by "word-of-mouth," without any written reminder. And the result here seems to have a charm and significance beyond the more usual "Shoe My Little Foot" offshoots of "Lass of Roch Royal."

Mrs. Basham's "Seafaring Man" had a very interesting old tune and style not previously found in print. Her husband, Bob Basham, sang this ballad to her when he came courting, which is an example of one way ballads continued to survive through use. Usually titled "The Silk Merchant's Daughter" in its infrequent American collection (often without tune), its plot resembles that of "Bonnie Annie" (Child #24) with some slight resemblance to "Brown Robyn's Confession" (Child #57).

"It Rained a Mist" is a ballad that Bertha Wright learned not from her family but rather from a man and woman who were traveling around taking tintype pictures when she was a child. It, too, is a Child ballad ("Sir Hugh, or, The Jew's Daughter," Child #155).

Lass of Roch Royal (Child #76)

As I walked out one morning in May
To hear the little birds sing,
I loaned my head to the nearest door,
To hear my true love say,

"Come in, my old true love,
  Sit down, sit down, for a moment's time.
  Oh, stay all night and take a rest,
  Take an early start in the morning."

"No, I can't come in and I can't sit down,
  For I have not a moment's time.
  I heard you had another true love,
  And your heart is no more mine."

"Oh, you will go off to some foreign land
  And there take sick and die.
  I'll not be there to cure your pain,
  Or to hear your mournful cry."

"Oh, who's goin' a' buy your brand-new shoes;
  Oh who's goin' a' glove your hands?
  And who's goin' a' kiss your red, rosy cheeks,
  When I'm in some foreign land?"

"My father will shoe my feet, my love,
  And my mother will glove my hands.
  And you may kiss my red, rosy, cheeks
  If ever you return again."

Seafaring Man

As I was a'walking up fair London Street,
  And a beauty, fair damsel had a chance for to meet.

"Oh, where are you going?" to the sailor said she.
"I am bound for New England, New England to see."

"'Tis a beauty, fair country. In vain I would go.
  But how I'm for to get there, it is more than I know."

"As I am no sails man; but a wayfaring man,
  As for your passage over, I will do all I can."

There was forty-five of them got on a long boat.
  And away over the ocean they all then did float.

'Til provision grew scanty and death's drawing nigh
  They all had for to cast lots to see who should die.

The tickets was made ready; put into a hat.
  Each man drew his ticket; each man drew his lot.

There was a fair damsel among all the rest.
  And she had to be murdered by the man she loved best.

"Hold on, loving porter, a minute or two,
  And see what I have come to by the loving of you."

"Before I could kill you, my poor heart would break.
  For the cause of your long life my own I'll forsake."

Up spoke this bold captain in the height of his men,
"There's the fewest of the people who would die for a friend."

They all was a'sailing when a gun they did hear.
  It revived their poor feelings and caused them to cheer.

Up spoke this bold captain. Says, "You may hold your hand.
  In less than one half an hour we'll be near ship or land."

They all was a'sailing on a swift rolling tide
'Til they come to the city all by the sea side.

There they took up housekeeping. He made her his wife.
  And I would ensure you they lived a sweet life.

It Rained a Mist (Sir Hugh, or, The Jew's Daughter, Child #155)

It rained a mist, it rained a mist,
It rained all over this town,
When two little children went out to play
To toss the ball around, around.
To toss the ball around.

At first too low and then too high
And then up over the wall.
And then into the maiden's room
Where no one was allowed to go, to go
Where no one was allowed to go.

Then at the door the maiden came,
All dressed in silk so fine,
Saying, "Come in, come in, you shall
    have your ball.
You shall have your ball again, again.
You shall have your ball again."

"I can't come in; I won't come in,
 Unless my playmates comes too.
 I've often heard of little ones coming in,
 And never coming out again, again.
 And never coming out again."

At first she showed them a red, rosy apple,
And then showed them a chain,
And then she showed them a diamond ring,
To entice the little one in, aye in.
To entice the little one in.

She took him by the lily-white hand,
And led him through the hall,
And then into the maiden's room
Where no one could hear his call, his call.
Where no one could hear his call.

She placed a napkin o'er his face,
And pinned it with a pin.
And then she taken her little pen-knife,
And taken his little heart in, aye in,
And taken his little heart in.

"Oh spare my life! Oh spare my life!
 Oh spare my life," he cried.
"And if I live to be a man,
 My treasure shall be aye thine, aye thine,
 My treasure shall be aye thine."

"Please place the prayer-book at my feet,
 The Bible at my head.
 And if my playmates call for me,
 You can tell them that I am dead, am dead,
 You can tell them that I am dead."

"The Ohio Canal" by J. W. Beattie, from The American Singer, Book Six, published by the American Book Company (1951)

5 John W. Beattie

The Ohio Canal

HURON COUNTY

I LIKED "THE Ohio Canal," composed by John W. Beattie, who was for many years the dean of the School of Music at Northwestern University in Illinois, from the day my kids brought it home. They sang it the way they learned it from *The American Singer,* their songbook in elementary school in Upper Arlington, Ohio.

Punchy and condensed, the song celebrates the time before the advent of the railroad in the late nineteenth century, when waterways in Ohio were critical for transportation of goods and people. It catches the same spirit of authentic old Ohio Canal songs kept alive through Captain Pearl R. Nye, whose "The Old Canal" or "Silver Ribbon" manages to include every stop on the Ohio and Erie Canal in some eighty verses.

Both Nye and Beattie composed "in the folk spirit" like Dan Emmett and Stephen Foster, whose works reflected folk material and, in turn, sometimes themselves became assimilated into folk music.

Margaret O. Moody in Chillicothe, Ohio, 1955. Photo by James W. Grimes

Although I frequently performed "The Ohio Canal"—especially on occasions like the old Canal Days celebrations at Roscoe Village near Coshocton—it is not part of my taped collection, which primarily is limited to items passed down in Ohio families for at least two generations.

However, a traditional canal song is in my tape collection, sung by Margaret O. Moody in Chillicothe, the county seat of Ross County. She knew there was lots more of her "Canal Song" or "Jolly Boatsman," and was very frustrated because she couldn't quite get it, but she did remember a couple of verses. Born in 1865, Mrs. Moody (who at age ninety recalled that her mother was "the prettiest jig dancer you ever saw in your life") grew up in Ross County and heard this song from the canalers themselves as she sat fishing on the bank:

> Oh, I am a jolly boatsman
> Drivin' is my trade.
> I can drive of a dark night,
> Be damned if I'm afraid.
> *Chorus:* Toodley do toodley do toodley do day.
>
> I hitched to the singletree
> And I drove it on the banks.
> And every time the whip cracked
> The old mule yanked.
> *Chorus*

As part of my research on canal songs, I corresponded with John Beattie about his "Ohio Canal" composition. Beattie told me that he had based the tune on several old tunes from his childhood in Norwalk, Ohio. The words came to him after his "vain attempt" to find a "former canal boater who lived in an old shack alongside what was left of the canal." Although Beattie never found this boatman, the experience inspired him to write his own song, which tracks the Ohio and Erie Canal from its northernmost part on Lake Erie to its southernmost on the Ohio River at Portsmouth.

Beattie coincidentally grew up in Norwalk with my father, Clarence Laylin; and Beattie's sisters, Anna and Blanche Beattie, were later friends and neighbors of mine in Granville, Ohio.

"Your parents would remember the Bragdon boys of Norwalk," Mr. Beattie wrote me in 1952. "I used to sing with them. At an age when boys of today would be running around in their dads' autos, we used to sit around a fire in a hut and sing."

The Ohio Canal
Lyrics and tune by John W. Beattie

Up the Cuyahoga, far as Akron,
Over locks aplenty to Coshocton,
Newark, Chillicothe, and down along the Scio,
Then to Portsmouth on the broad Ohio.

Chorus:
Float her high, boys, float her low!
Through the locks, boys, ease her slow!
Always heading for the valley we'll be seeing by and by,
For we'll keep the boats a-running if we pump Lake Erie dry!

Dozing on the deck in pleasant sunshine,
While the horses drag along the tow-line,
Waking from the dreaming of cargo we are hauling
"Bridge ahead!" I hear somebody calling.
Chorus

Henry Lawrence Beecher with the author in his Mt. Vernon, Ohio, home, 1953. Photo by James W. Grimes

6 Henry Lawrence Beecher

The Mouse and Plum Cake · Ohio Guards · The Old Sow

LICKING COUNTY

A REMARKABLE GENTLEMAN, a lovely spirit, and a fine ballad singer, Henry Lawrence Beecher of Mt. Vernon, Ohio, had wonderful, wonderful songs—including Child ballads, like "Robin Hood Rescuing Three Squires," that I've gotten lots of Brownie points for in folklore—ones forgotten in England today.

You see, that's the thing: people couldn't bring material possessions here, but they could bring songs. And they clung to them, and they told their children about them, and that's why the tradition faded in the British Isles—in England, Scotland, and Ireland—but remained strong in America.

A widower in his mid-sixties when I met him, Mr. Beecher had taught engineering at Swarthmore College and Cornell University before coming to Knox County, where he worked some forty years as an engineer. He had been blinded in a freak accident some ten years earlier when he got hit in the head by a basketball while refereeing at a game for the YMCA in Mt. Vernon. However, he remained active in numerous Knox County music, athletic, and civic affairs, as well as in his work as a consulting engineer, and he became an active member of the Ohio Folklore Society.

I recorded Mr. Beecher singing his traditional family songs at his lovely house, full of tangible heirlooms, in Mt. Vernon. He was descended from the Beechers (as in Henry Ward Beecher and Harriet Beecher Stowe) and Hancocks (John). The Hancocks came from Luray, Virginia, around 1830 to Luray, Ohio, in Licking County, because that's where the Erie Canal crossed the National Road. That was supposed to be the good place, and it was a good place.

Both sides of his family were musical, and their songs were traditional for several generations in Licking County. Beecher traced most of his songs to his mother, Emmeline Hancock Beecher, who was one of ten children. He recalled that when he was a youngster in Licking County, he heard a lot of singing around the house—particularly at the home of his Grandfather Hancock:

> It was just an everyday habit to stand around the organ and sing after a meal. If they were too busy during the week, why they never missed Sunday noon, anyway, or following the Sunday dinner. I heard a lot of songs by one or more of them that I have never seen in print. I have looked for them many times in various sources.

Beecher said the family's best singer was his uncle Jim Hancock, who had a dramatic tenor voice. A veteran of the Civil War, he was much in demand at large conventions, particularly at encampments of the G.A.R. (Grand Old Army) in Columbus.

Beecher was very interested in adding his "family songs" to my collection and wanted to learn what he could about them. After I got home from our recording session in which he sang "Saw a Sparrow," he called me long-distance (which we didn't do so much in those days) to ask:

"Did I say flap jack or slap jack—I want to make sure that I got that right."

I was able to tell Mr. Beecher that his "Saw a Sparrow" (which ends "we'll all slap jack and be happy here below") was a version of "The Liar's Song," a Scots drinking song from the time of Shakespeare. I mean it is that old. And within a year I collected that same song—different tune—from a dulcimer player in southeast Ohio, Ken Ward.

Beecher referred to his "The Mouse and Plum Cake"—taught to him by his mother—as a "children lesson song." A version of "Mouse and Plum Cake" very similar to Mr. Beecher's later was sent to me by Granville historian William T. Utter. He discovered the song in the Granville library in a folded leaflet titled "Singing-School Songs." Dr. Utter wrote that the leaflet had been prepared by Chaplain Joseph Little for use in his services during the Civil War.

A favorite song of Mr. Beecher's father, Henry Lyman Beecher, was "Ohio Guards" or "You're Wanted for a Hundred Days," as Mr. Beecher called it from the first line in the first verse. "Ohio Guards" is obviously a parody of an old Irish soldier song, "The Battle of the Boyne," dating from 1690, whose tune, "The Boyne Water," is indicated in early American songsters. But the tune is even more similar to a bawdy parody, "The Boiling Water," or "King William's Daughter," which is a song that my father, Clarence Laylin, learned as a student at Ohio State in the early twentieth century.

Mr. Beecher never taped his "There Was an Old Sow" but sang it to me long-distance over the phone, mailed the text, and later approved my arrangement with dulcimer and my performance of the song. It is just a cute little song about baby pigs and their mama, the sow.

Something that is too fancy, too wordy, you suspect is not traditional. In a traditional song, you can anticipate the rhyme; it is something very easy to learn and hard to forget. Sometimes you wish you could! But there was a phrase in "There Was an Old Sow" that intrigued me: "fay-lo-di-see" that describes the fate of the piggies. From the context, I thought it must mean "fatal disease," but wasn't sure and neither was Mr. Beecher. I consulted my law-professor father who suggested looking it up in an unabridged dictionary. There we found "felo de se"—a Norman-French-English legal term for suicide. Mr. Beecher was very much interested in that.

"The Mouse and Plum Cake" as sung by Henry Lawrence Beecher. Notation by the author

The Mouse and Plum Cake

A mouse found a beautiful piece of plum cake,
The sweetest, the richest that mortals could make.
All heavied with citron and laden with spice,
All covered with sugar as sparkling as ice.

"My, my!" cried the mouse, as his eyes gleamed with glee.
"What a treasure I've found, what a prize it will be."
And so he kept quiet and held the cake fast
While his hungry young playmates went scampering past.

He nibbled and nibbled and panted, but still
He kept gulping it down till he made himself ill.
He swallowed it all and it's easy to guess
He soon was so ill that he groaned with distress.

His parents heard him and as he grew worse,
They called for the doctor; they made him rehearse
How he'd eaten the cake to the very last crumb
Without giving his playmates and relatives some.

So little children a lesson may take,
And older ones too from the mouse and the cake:
Not to be selfish with what you may gain,
Or the best of your pleasures may turn into pain.

Ohio Guards

You are wanted for one hundred days.
Be ready in one minute.
So General Cowen's order says.
There must be something in it.
Ho, lads untackle from the plow.
Unharness all the horses.
Quick, climb the saddle on them now,
To join the Union forces.

Chorus:
To arms, ye guards, Ohio calls;
And louder calls the Nation;
Oh, then arise ere freedom falls,
Arise and save the Nation!

So, farewell, Bub; good-bye, sweet Sis,
I have no time to tarry.
Yet time enough to snatch one kiss
From thee, my darling Mary.

The Old Sow

There was an old sow who lived in a sty,
And three little piggies had she.
She waddled around saying "Oink, oink, oink!"
While the little ones said "Wee, wee."

"My dear little brothers," said one of the brats.
"My dear little brothers," said he.
"Let's waddle around saying 'Oink, oink, oink.'
It's so childish to say 'Wee, wee.'"

Then these little piggies grew skinny and lean,
And skinny they very well be,
From trying so hard to say "Oink, oink, oink,"
When they only could say "Wee, wee."

Well, these little piggies, they up and they died.
They died from that felo de se.
From trying too hard to say "Oink, oink, oink,"
When they only could say "Wee, wee."

Now here is the moral of this sad little song,
A moral that's easy to see.
Don't waddle around saying "Oink, Oink, Oink,"
When you only can say "Wee, wee."

John M. Bodiker in Columbus, Ohio, late 1950s. Photo by James W. Grimes

7 John M. Bodiker

Gypsy Davey · Lady and Laddie · Jack and His Kind Master
The Substitute · The Jealous Sister

**PAULDING
COUNTY**

I KNEW THE FIRST evening we went to call on John Bodiker at his home in Columbus that I had struck pay dirt. Here was a real singer. The highlight that night was his singing of his mother's beautiful tune to a full version of "Gypsy Davey."

Bodiker was seventy-nine years old when we met in the spring of 1957 through Ben Hayes, the columnist at the *Columbus Citizen*. Ben had mentioned my work collecting songs during a talk he gave to the Senior Citizens Center where Bodiker was an active member, and later president. Bodiker told Ben he'd be glad to give me a ballad he knew—"a song brought over from old England."

Bodiker sang songs he had learned growing up in the 1880s in rural Paulding County in northwestern Ohio. He sang in a sweet, strong voice with excellent diction, but curiously (and somewhat typically of traditional singers) had not thought of himself as a singer. At the Senior Citizens Center, he played fiddle at informal gatherings and was known for his dancing. He danced several times a week, and often did exhibition schottische with his regular partner, Mrs. John Dawson.

Jimmie and I invited Bodiker to dinner the very next night after our get-acquainted interview, and he arrived with over ten songs typed up and ready to go, some of which he had illustrated with clever drawings. This was the first time he had written any of his songs down.

Over the next fifteen years, John Bodiker became an ideal contributor. He taped for my collection some sixty-six items, of which twenty-two are rare. His contributions include seven full texts and tunes of Child ballads, two full Child tunes and fragment texts, and four Child variants; fifteen other British ballad survivals; and thirty-eight indigenous items including three historical songs, children's and nursery songs, minstrel songs, railroad songs, a hymn, a sea chantey, fiddle tunes, recitations, and tongue twisters. He had never seen any of these in print, and some had never been previously collected.

I always enjoyed John's saying, "If only I could go courting again, I could remember the songs better."

It was during our second evening together that Bodiker began to recall his bawdy songs (or as he called them, "ribalds," pronounced "rye-balds"). These songs were of special interest to me, many reflecting medieval and Renaissance origins in their archaic words and tunes.

"Lady and Laddie"—which is a fine medieval British ballad—Bodiker said he learned from "a couple of drunks" when he was a boy, later on picking up more verses in Louisville, Kentucky. "Jack and His Kind Master," also possibly medieval, Bodiker also learned as a boy: "Old fellas would get out, you know, and get a bunch of young fellas and sing 'em them songs . . . they had a drink or two and they'd do any old thing."

"The Substitute" Bodiker said he heard even his father singing "out behind the barn." Often collected as "The Tarry Sailor" or "Jack the Jolly Tar," the ballad in Bodiker's version has a lovely old tune, and the story has been found in chapbook versions in straight prose form as "The Squire and the Farm Servant."

Bodiker was reticent at first about sharing his bawdy material. He would sometimes introduce a song with a phrase like, "You know in the old days, the lords went wenching. . . ." Jimmie's good-natured presence and encouragement no doubt helped, but—as so often was the case with my contributors—my own singing also helped "prime the pump" and establish rapport.

John M. Bodiker at eighty-one years of age traveled from Columbus to sing his family's songs at the National Folk Festival in Nashville, Tennessee, in 1959. Columbus Citizen, *Scripps-Howard Newspapers/Grandview Heights Public Library/ Photohio.org*

Many of the oldest and most interesting of Bodiker's songs were learned from his father and mother, both of whom were of pioneer Ohio families. Some of these ballads may have come into Bodiker's extensive British traditional repertoire during his family's (seventeenth-century) stopover in Holland "during the religious troubles" en route from Scotland to America. In their youth, Bodiker's parents sang some of their songs at school and at "literaries," but by the time Bodiker was born the songs were sung mainly at home.

"They always had their mouths open singing and were great at it," Bodiker said of his parents.

His mother's "Gypsy Davey," usually known as "The Gypsy Laddie," is a version notable for the beauty of its tune and some unusual phrases, as well as for its story plot, in which the young lord not only catches his wife but also kills her lover, Gypsy Davey.

Another of the famous British ballads Bodiker learned from his mother was "The Jealous Sister," usually known as "The Two Sisters." Bodiker sang it slowly, as his mother had.

Bodiker's maternal great-grandmother, who died when Bodiker was five, was born in Scotland in 1794. Bodiker remembered that she was proud of her family's songs and ballads and that she often recalled, usually whenever the family "put on airs," that she spent her wedding night dancing barefoot on the puncheon floor, dressed in linsey-woolsey.

The interesting thing about Bodiker was that when I met him he had not sung his family songs since he was a young man. Perhaps this had to do with his father's death when Bodiker was only thirteen years old, which vastly changed his young life. Bodiker's paternal grandfather had given the land for the chapel from which the town where he was born got its name, Blue Crick Chapel. But after his father died, Bodiker's mother was forced to sell their farm and move to Lima, Ohio, where she opened a boardinghouse to support her six children. John, the oldest, went to work as a hired farm laborer. He later became a brass and iron molder, retiring at age seventy-five.

However, his self-education was lifelong, thanks to his amazing memory, his interest in people and current events, his poems (many of which were in the form of old ballads; some took prizes at the state fair), his avid reading (especially of history and classical literature), and his humor. He was charming and had a cosmopolitan urbanity. At my party gatherings, for instance, he could hold his own with "folk experts" like Bascom Lamar Lunsford, distinguished and gutsy North Carolina folklorist and ballad singer. Bodiker also developed a wonderful friendship through the Ohio Folklore Society with A. B. Graham, a founder of the 4-H Clubs and also a contributor to my collection.

A fine, natural singer, Bodiker's own enjoyment of his songs and the stories they told, or the fun in them, made him effective with audiences; and he became one of the favorites at annual Ohio Folklore Society jamborees. When I was unable because of a schedule conflict to perform in 1959 at the National Folk Festival in Nashville, I sent then eighty-one-year-old John Bodiker in my stead. I recommended him to the festival's National Advisory Committee, of which I was a member, as one of the Midwest's best real folksingers.

On his return, Bodiker told Ben Hayes in a column that appeared May 17, 1959, in the *Columbus Citizen:* "I sang and danced all over Nashville. The dancing sure gave me two hot dogs. I'm still a little fuzzed after the big to-do."

In his report on his Nashville experience, Bodiker wrote that among the people he met was Fiddler Beers of Montana: "I had a short talk with him and he told me that he didn't believe in pulling any punches in Folklore even though some parts may seem a little rough. We must preserve Folklore as we know it. And I agree with him."

I was glad to learn that among the songs Bodiker sang on stage in Nashville was the one he sang the first night we met—his mother's beautiful "Gypsy Davey."

John Bodiker died in March 1973, shortly before his ninety-fifth birthday. He was a very intelligent and dear person and friend.

Gypsy Davey
(The Gypsy Laddie, Child #200)

A young man came singing down the glen,
And he sang so very merrily.
He sang till he made the forest ring,
And he charmed the heart of a lady.

Chorus:
Rum-tittle tum tum, tittle tittle tum,
Rum-tittle tum tum dadey.
He sang till he made the forest ring,
And he charmed the heart of a lady.
(Repeat last two lines of each verse)

Young lady tripping down the stairs
With her hair combed out so wavy,
A bottle of wine in one fair hand,
A gift to Gypsy Davey.
Chorus

"Would you forsake your house and land;
Would you forsake your baby?
Would you forsake your own dear lord,
And go with the Gypsy Davey?"
Chorus

"Yes, I'll forsake my house and land.
Yes, I'll forsake my baby.
Yes, I'll forsake my own dear lord,
And go with the Gypsy Davey."
Chorus

"Last night I slept in a nice warm bed
And in my arms my baby.
Tonight I sleep on the cold, damp ground
In the arms of Gypsy Davey."
Chorus

"Last night I slept in a warm feather bed
And my own dear lord beside me.
Tonight I sleep on the cold, damp ground,
With the howling wolves all 'round me."
Chorus

Young lord came home quite late at night
Inquiring for his lady.
But the servants gave him this reply,
"She's gone with the Gypsy Davey."
Chorus

He rode 'til he came to the riverside
In a little grove so shady.
And there he slew the gypsy lad
That had ran away with his lady.
Chorus

Lady and Laddie

A lady loved a laddie,
A boy of low degree.
She came of noble lineage
And could boast her pedigree.

Chorus:
Sing whack fall loll, foll de roll,
Whack foll loll de raye.

Her husband was so aged
That when he went to bed,
He told her love was wicked,
And she'd love her God instead.
Chorus

Said she, "My lordly husband,
If I may be so bold,
I do crave some carnal loving
And will pray when I get old."
Chorus

So she sent a note to laddie
Asking, "What am I to do?
His lordship does not love me,
And I only think of you."
Chorus

He answered, "Dearest lady,
Your proposal I do dread.
If your lordship should hear about us
He would you and I behead."
Chorus

"Jack and His Kind Master" as sung by John M. Bodiker. Notation by the author

She answered, "Dearest laddie,
Please do not be unkind.
For I have brewed a potion
That will make his lordship blind."
Chorus

She poured the potion in some wine,
And his lordship drank it all.
Then he cried, "My dearest lady,
I cannot see at all, at all."
Chorus

She led her lord unto his bed
And stroked his hair so gray
Saying, "Go to sleep, my darling
While I with my priest do pray."
Chorus

Her laddie dressed in priestly robes
Within the castle halls,
Gave the lady absolution
On a bench along the wall.
Chorus

Jack and His Kind Master

(***): At this point, Bodiker made an
embarrassed laugh or a tongue-click.

Oh, Jack and his kind master the wager they did play.
The one that had the longest *(***)* the wager had to pay.
Sing tithery wire away; sing tithery wire away.

They down with their britches and they measured an inch about,
And Jackie beat his master by six inches at the snout.
Sing tithery wire away; sing tithery wire away.

The maid being out, she thought she was to blame.
She went right up to the house and told it to the dame.
Sing tithery wire away; sing tithery wire away.

The old woman she went to the barn, some hen eggs for to hunt.
While strolling around among the straw, a mouse ran up her *(***)*.
Sing tithery wire away; sing tithery wire away.

She stepped to the door and she cried both loud and shrill,
'Til the old man overheard her; he was flouring at the mill.
Sing tithery wire away; sing tithery wire away.

He came to the house just as hard as he could walk,
Saying, "What's the matter, my dear old wife; I thought I heard you talk."
Sing tithery wire away; sing tithery wire away.

"A mouse ran up my belly-gut and vicious he does gnaw,
And if we don't soon get him out, my bowels he will chaw."
Sing tithery wire away; sing tithery wire away.

He took her by her slender waist; he laid her on the floor.
He couldn't reach that mouse's tail by six inches and some more.
Sing tithery wire away; sing tithery wire away.

He stepped to the door and he cried both loud and shrill
'Til Jackie overheard him; he was plowing on a hill.
Sing tithery wire away; sing tithery wire away.

Jackie came to the house just as fast as he could ride,
Saying, "What's the matter, my dear old boss; I thought I heard you cry."
Sing tithery wire away; sing tithery wire away.

"A mouse ran up wife's belly-gut and vicious he does gnaw.
If we don't soon get him out, her bowels he will chaw."
Sing tithery wire away; sing tithery wire away.

Jackie took her by her slender waist and laid her on the ground.
With every jerk and half a jerk, he turned that mouse around.
Sing tithery wire away; sing tithery wire away.

The old man standing by her side, with a pitch fork in his hand,
Swearing vengeance on that god-damned mouse, if he ever came to land.
Sing tithery wire away; sing tithery wire away.

The old woman being kind, she had hid one up her sleeve.
When Jackie came and (***), she give the mouse a heave.
Sing tithery wire away; sing tithery wire away.

The little mouse jumped down; it went running along the wall.
The old man struck at him a hell of a jab, and he missed it after all.
Sing tithery wire away; sing tithery wire away.

The Substitute

As Jack was in a garden walking,
He overheard his squire and a maid a'talking.
The squire said, "Promise me, my dove,
That this very night we two shall love."
To my foddle riddle rido, to my foddle riddle ri.

"I will tie a string around my finger,
And put one end out of the window.
You'll come up and pull the string,
And I'll come down and let you in."
To my foddle riddle rido, to my foddle riddle ri.

Now Jack this maiden did admire,
With her ruby lips and eyes of fire.
Within himself he planned that day
To rob that eagle off his prey.
To my foddle riddle rido, to my foddle riddle ri.

That night while stars were brightly shining,
And the maid was on her bed reclining,
With cord from finger hung outside,
For the squire to claim his unwed bride.
Sing foddle riddle rido, sing a foddle riddle ri.

Now, Jack the lackey was approaching;
He on the squire's conquest encroaching.
He said, "What's yours is mine as well,
It's my night in heaven and yours of hell."
Sing foddle riddle rido, sing a foddle riddle ri.

In the dark shadows Jack did linger,
To find the string tied to her finger.
He found it; gave three pulls or more.
She came and led him to her door.
Sing foddle riddle rido, sing a foddle riddle ri.

She whispered, "Make it sound I pray,
Or you my sire will surely slay.
I notice you have ridden hard.
You smell of horse and stable yard."
Sing foddle riddle rido, sing a foddle riddle ri.

The squire he came, and he did linger,
But found no cord outside her window.
He stayed until the light of day
Did warn him to no longer stay.
Sing foddle riddle rido, sing a foddle riddle ri.

The next morning she did awaken,
She looked like a maid forsaken.
There lay Jack with a dirty shirt,
His hands and face begrimed with dirt.
Sing foddle riddle rido, sing a foddle riddle ri.

She said to Jack, "What will I do?
I want the squire and I don't want you."
Jack says, "I've got enough and I won't tell,
So wed the squire and go to hell."
Sing foddle riddle rido, sing a foddle riddle ri.

The Jealous Sister
(The Two Sisters, Child #10)

A little old widow lived by the seashore,
    Bow-Down.
A little old widow lived by the seashore,
The bow was bent for me.
A little old widow lived by the seashore,
And she had daughters three or four.

Refrain:
That'll be true, true to my lover,
If my lover is true to me.

The youngest daughter did have a beau,
    Bow-Down.
The youngest daughter did have a beau,
The bow was bent for me.
The youngest daughter did have a beau,
And the oldest couldn't get any to go.
Refrain

He gave to the youngest a beaver hat,
    Bow-Down.
He gave to the youngest a beaver hat,
The bow was bent for me.
He gave his youngest a beaver hat,
And the oldest said she didn't like that.
Refrain

He gave to the youngest a diamond ring,
    Bow-Down.
He gave to the youngest a diamond ring,
The bow was bent for me.
He gave to the youngest a diamond ring,
And the eldest didn't get anything.
Refrain

"Oh, sister, dear sister, let's take a walk,"
    Bow-Down.
"Oh, sister, dear sister, let's take a walk,"
The bow was bent for me.
"Oh, sister, dear sister, let's take a walk,
And view the land as we do talk."
Refrain

They walked beside the millpond brim,
    Bow-Down.
They walked beside the millpond brim,
The bow was bent for me.
They walked beside the millpond brim,
And the oldest pushed the youngest one in.
Refrain

"Oh sister, dear sister, please lend me your hand,"
    Bow-Down.
"Oh sister, dear sister, please lend me your hand,"
The bow was bent for me.
"Oh sister, dear sister, please lend me your hand,
And you may have my lover and land."
Refrain

"I will neither lend you my hand or my glove,"
    Bow-Down.
"I will neither lend you my hand or my glove,"
The bow was bent for me.
"I will neither lend you my hand or my glove
To gain the heart of your own true love."
Refrain

She floated down to the miller's brook,
    Bow-Down.
She floated down to the miller's brook,
The bow was bent for me.
She floated down to the miller's brook,
And the miller, he caught her on his
    own mill hook.
Refrain

The miller was hung on his own mill gate,
    Bow-Down.
The miller was hung on his own mill gate,
The bow was bent for me.
The miller was hung on his own mill gate
For the murder of her sister Kate.
Refrain

8 Paul Bogatay

The Sea Crab

PAUL BOGATAY CONTRIBUTED to my collection the famous bawdy ballad "The Sea Crab," which he called "The Fisherman"—a rare item indeed.

We first heard Bogatay sing "The Sea Crab," with its jaunty tune or "air" and whistling refrain, at a party at our house on the occasion of a visit to Columbus by poet, author, and folklorist Carl Sandburg. Bogatay's singing was part of the fun encouraged by Sandburg, who also entertained us with some bawdy songs and stories of his own.

I didn't manage to get Bogatay's version of "The Sea Crab" on tape that evening. However, about a year later I did tape-record him singing the song, accompanying himself on banjo, with his wife, Hennie, joining him on the vocals.

"The Sea Crab" dates back to seventeenth-century England. As Gershon Legman wrote in his article, "The Bawdy Song . . . in Fact and in Print," this song should have been a Child ballad, but for the prudery in folk music scholarship and presentation that discouraged the publishing of collected materials involving sex and other "unmentionable" facts of life well into the twentieth century.

An eminent ceramic artist, Paul taught for many years at Ohio State University, where he was a colleague of Jimmie's in the fine arts department. Paul said that his version of "The Sea Crab" was a fraternity song he learned while a student at the Cleveland School of Art in the 1920s.

I kept most of my bawdy material from the ears of my young children. However, they managed to pick up on "The Sea Crab," and it was a favorite.

The Sea Crab

"Fisherman, fisherman, I wish you very well, *(whistle)*
Fisherman, fisherman, I wish you very well,
Have you any sea crabs for to sell?"
Singing dingie-eye-dingie-eye-dee.

"Yes, sir, yes, sir, one or two or three, *(whistle)*
Yes, sir, yes, sir, one or two or three,
And the best damn sea crabs you ever did see."
Singing dingie-eye-dingie-eye-dee.

Oh, grab that sea crab by the backbone, *(whistle)*
Grab that sea crab by the backbone,
And he lugged and he tugged 'til he got the bastard home.
Singing dingie-eye-dingie-eye-dee.

And when he got home, his wife was asleep, *(whistle)*
When he got home, his wife was asleep,
So he put him in the piss pot for to keep.
Singing dingie-eye-dingie-eye-dee.

Wife got up and thought she had to do, *(whistle)*
Wife got up and thought she had to do,
And the damned old sea crab got her by the flue.
Singing dingie-eye-dingie-eye-dee.

"Old man, old man, sure as you're born, *(whistle)*
Old man, old man, sure as you're born,
There's a devil in the piss pot; got me on his horn."
Singing dingie-eye-dingie-eye-dee.

"Old woman, old woman, can't you let a fart, *(whistle)*
Old woman, old woman, can't you let a fart,
And blow that sea crab all apart?"
Singing dingie-eye-dingie-eye-dee.

"Old man, old man, I can't fart a bit, *(whistle)*
Old man, old man, I can't fart a bit,
But I'll fill that sea crab's eyes full of shit."
Singing dingie-eye-dingie-eye-dee.

Now my story's done, and I'll sing you no more, *(whistle)*
Now my story's done, and I'll sing you no more.
There's an apple up my asshole and you can have the core.
Singing dingie-eye-dingie-eye-dee.

Dolleah Church at her Crazy Quilt Antique Shop in Columbus, Ohio, mid-1950s. Photo by James W. Grimes. Anne Grimes Collection, American Folklife Center, Library of Congress

9 Dolleah Church

Wordplay: Riddle, Tongue Twister, Tricky Talk

MEIGS
COUNTY

MRS. DOLLEAH "DOLLY" CHURCH owned the Crazy Quilt Antique Shop on East Mound Street in downtown Columbus. Active in the Ohio Folklore Society, she knew a lot of song fragments and gave me a lot of leads to other contributors, especially in Meigs County, Ohio, where she grew up and later spent her summers—and in other areas of Ohio as well.

Some of Dolly's songs she learned from her father, who had been a steamboat river man and coal miner before he took up farming in Pomeroy, Ohio, on the Ohio River.

Bunny with Dulcimer. Drawing by Dolleah Church courtesy of the Grimes family

When Jimmie and I tape-recorded Dolly in Columbus in 1954, she told us: "I was the only one born in Pomeroy, and the rest of us was born in the country. I used to kid the rest of them and tell them, 'I come from the city.'"

Dolly also knew a lot about many areas of folklore, including home remedies, from growing up in Meigs County. She made Jimmie and me laugh with her wordplay, including her "tricky talk" and riddles. I suggested some of these may have come out of spelling lessons at school—that is, learning by syllable.

"Well," she said, "we sang and spoke pieces but just among ourselves—we'd tell them probably going or coming from school."

Dolly had a great zest for life captured in this description of her by *Columbus Citizen* columnist Ben Hayes:

Mrs. Church bubbled like a pot of noodles on the boil. She spouted riddles, superstitions, remedies, ghost tales and ridiculous family anecdotes of southern Ohio flavor. . . . She was known in Columbus as 'Queen of the Junk Dealers'—a self-imposed title. A rummage-sale addict, she swept through the Central Market district with 19th Century grandeur. Her head was erect; her auburn hair piled high, her friendly eye alert. Along the doodad trail, she was the infallible bird dog.

We all adored Dolly. She was just a very special person—and uninhibited, oh boy, was she. She thought she could see an aura around Tris Coffin (then president of the Ohio Folklore Society) and told me I was "an old soul."

She was always giving us things—like the drawing she made for me of a bunny playing the dulcimer. She drew things for the children, too, and she and Jimmie shared an expertise in "junk," which she defined as antiques less than a hundred years old.

My children loved visiting Dolly at her shop and seeing all of her treasures. She lived in a back room with her cat Paisley, who played the piano, and you were greatly honored to be invited back there. She really was like one of the family.

Wordplay

Riddle:
My mother sent me to borrow your mother's
Himble bow, hamble bow, iron bow,
Three-legged lillickle lallickle, horticka-jig.
(What is it? Answer: A spinning wheel. Spoken fast, the nonsense syllables are meant to sound like a spinning wheel in action.)

Tongue Twister:
Abominable bee with its tail cut off.
(This phrase she broke down and repeated syllable by syllable in various patterns. Dolly was a little rusty on this one. As she herself said, "Boy, it gets busy. You spell it out in syllables, and you'll catch on to it.")

Tricky Talk or Double Talk:
Dolly spoke in her "tricky talk" a phrase so fast as to be incomprehensible. When asked what she had said, she enunciated: "I went upstairs. I looked out to the window. I saw the fox in the field. I called the dog to run the fox out of the field."

The author performing at presentation ceremonies at the Rubicon Homestead in Dayton, Ohio, 1953. Photographer unknown

10 Governor James M. Cox

Harding Campaign Song

MONTGOMERY
COUNTY

IN THE FALL OF 1953, I sang in Dayton, Ohio, at the gorgeous old homestead called "Rubicon," when it was donated to the city by Jefferson Patterson, a career diplomat from a prominent Montgomery County family. Built in 1816, the house had been in his pioneer family for generations. After the dedication ceremonies, a very beautiful older lady came up to me and said, "Do you ever do private programs?"

It turned out she was the wife of James M. Cox, who had been governor of Ohio before running on the Democratic ticket for president of the United States in 1920 against Warren G. Harding, another Ohioan. The Cox children and grandchildren were all coming for Thanksgiving, and Mrs. Cox wanted me to entertain their party with songs of Ohio.

It happened that there was a big blizzard on Thanksgiving eve, and my train was delayed, so it was late when I arrived in Dayton. I was met at the station by the family chauffeur, who whisked me off to their beautiful home, called "Trailsend." Mrs. Cox had several friends in, as well as the family, and she had everything arranged for me to be a surprise.

Of course, Governor Cox was terribly interesting and smart. He started quizzing me on certain things that I happened to know, so we just hit it off fine. And he had known my grandfather, Lewis Cass Laylin, who was also a politician who had campaigned in every county in the state, so their paths had crossed.

I sang for Governor Cox a song that is not traditional but that I remembered being sung by the Republican Men's Glee Club in 1920 during the Harding-Cox campaign—and later by other Republican singing groups and by my own family, who mostly sang it for fun. He was so tickled by it.

They wanted me to stay the night, but I had to get back for my own family Thanksgiving, so they finally arranged for me to go home on the milk train. It was just me and the crew—no other passengers—and we sat in the caboose. We sang all the way, and I got some good railroad songs.

Harding Campaign Song
I'm from Ohio, dear old Ohio,
Oh, there's nothing quite so fine
As that Buckeye state of mine.

I'm from Ohio, dear old Ohio,
'Round my home my heartstrings twine.

It's the land of Grant and Sherman,
McKinley, Garfield, too,
And you'll hear from President Harding
Before this year is through.

If anyone can bait him, it is Jimmie Cox from Dayton,
For he's from Ohio, too!

11 Walter W. Dixon

The Pious Little Men

WALTER W. DIXON of Rochester, New York, sang a lovely, old Shaker song, "The Pious Little Men."

It was rare by the 1950s to find anyone who traditionally remembered any of the songs of the Shakers. Mr. Dixon's singing of the song was a real find, previously unrecorded.

A Rochester businessman, Mr. Dixon shared his song with me after I gave a program in Rochester for the Rochester Ad Club in 1955. Dixon learned it as a child from his maternal grandmother, Harriet Wakelee Hall, who was born on Christmas Day in 1823. The daughter of a pioneer merchant of Rochester, she heard the song as a girl, possibly at the Shaker community in Sodus, some thirty miles east of Rochester.

"I understand it was sung as the Shaker men marched around the room," Mr. Dixon wrote to me.

Advocates of communal living, celibacy, and worship through singing and dancing, the Shakers were an interesting religious sect and also important in the history of the times. The Shaker communities reached their height before the Civil War, and then went into decline as their population aged. Shaker hymns also changed as their unaccompanied, unharmonized singing, marching, and dancing exercises were influenced by the revival folk-hymns.

Shaker religious dance ended completely by 1871; melodeons were brought into the meetinghouses and conventional hymn singing was generally adopted. The last Shaker community in the Midwest—South Union, in Kentucky—was dissolved in 1922.

My interest in the Shakers and their music began in 1952 following a program I gave for an alumnae group at Ohio State University in Columbus. I sang Dan Emmett's "Boatman's Dance," which triggered a memory in a woman who was in the audience named Elizabeth Frost. Her father had been a lawyer for the Union Village Shaker community near Lebanon, Ohio, where she and other children, who were not Shakers, sang this song about their Shaker neighbors, to the tune of "Boatman's Dance:"

> The Shakers dance,
> The Shakers sing,
> The Shakers are in motion.
> But whether they dance
> Or whether they sing,
> It always suits their notion.

Among the people I enjoyed knowing through my Shaker research was Carolyn Piercy, a fellow member of the Ohio Historical

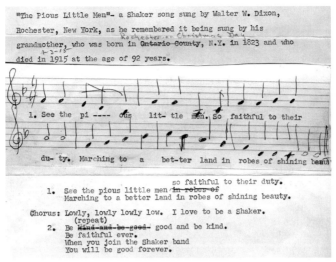

"The Pious Little Men"- a Shaker song sung by Walter W. Dixon,
Rochester, New York, as he remembered it being sung by his
grandmother, who was born in Ontario County, N.Y. in 1823 and who
died in 1915 at the age of 92 years.

1. See the pi---ous lit-tle men. So faithful to their
du-ty. Marching to a bet-ter land in robes of shining beauty.

so faithful to their duty.
1. See the pious little men in robes of
   Marching to a better land in robes of shining beauty.

Chorus: Lowly, lowly lowly low. I love to be a Shaker.
        (repeat)
2. Be kind and be good good and be kind.
   Be faithful ever.
   When you join the Shaker band
   You will be good forever.

"The Pious Little Men" as sung by Walter W. Dixon. Notation by the author

Society, who was the founder and guiding spirit of the Shaker Historical Society of Shaker Heights near Cleveland, Ohio. Shaker Heights had been the site of one of four Shaker communities in the state. The first and parent community of western Shakerdom was Union, near Lebanon, Ohio, established in 1805. Watervliet and Whitewater were also in the southwestern part of the state. All four were gone by 1913.

I met other people who remembered their Shaker neighbors, but none of them could sing me any Shaker songs—until Walter Dixon. His well-sung "Pious Little Men" has a subtle simplicity and rhythmic spontaneity that, to me, seems a unique survival of early "Shaker Highs" or "Quick Meetings."

The Pious Little Men
See the pious little men
So faithful to their duty,
Marching to a better land
In robes of shining beauty.

Chorus:
Lowly, lowly, lowly, low,
I love to be a Shaker.
Lowly, lowly, lowly, low,
I love to be a Shaker.

Be kind and be good;
Be faithful ever.
If you join the Shaker band,
You will be good forever.
Chorus

Bob White with the author in Wilkesville, Ohio, 1955. Photo by James W. Grimes. Smithsonian Institution Collections, National Museum of American History, Behring Center

12 Dulcerine Players of Southeastern Ohio

Bob White, Ken Ward, Lilly McGhee Ward Swick, Charles Ralston

The Liar's Song

VINTON, MEIGS, JACKSON AND GALLIA COUNTIES

JIMMIE AND I were dulcimer hunting in the southeastern Ohio counties of Vinton, Meigs, Jackson, and Gallia—lovely, hilly country—when we discovered a nest of dulcimer lore. That was the day we met Bob White of Wilkesville in Vinton County; who sent us to see Ken Ward and his mother, Lilly Ward Swick, near Bidwell in adjacent Gallia County; who in turn sent us to see a neighbor, Charles Ralston. They all played the dulcimer, or as they and others in that area most often called the instrument, the "dulcerine."

Active in the Holiness Church, Bob White played only hymns and religious music on his dulcimer. I tape-recorded his playing of

Bob White with his son in Wilkesville, Ohio, 1955. Photo by James W. Grimes. Smithsonian Institution Collections, National Museum of American History, Behring Center

"I'll Settle the Question," an old hymn that was still popular in the church at that time. He got his very fine dulcimer from his father, Wilbur "Wib" White, who played more worldly, play-party tunes like "Turkey in the Straw" and "Arkansas Traveler."

Bob tuned his instrument just as his father had taught him: sol-sol-sol-do. But instead of the traditional syllables, he intoned: "Pick–Up–Cow–Dung." We enjoyed that so much we asked him to demonstrate again, and Bob joined in our laughter. His young son wanted to know what was so amusing: "You just forget it, son," he said. "I'll tell you some other time."

Next we went to the home of Ken Ward on his farm near Bidwell in Gallia County. University-educated and a Grange leader who taught school before becoming a cattle farmer, Ken was well known in southeastern Ohio as a musician who played both dulcimer and fiddle at community events. Ken said:

> There is a kind of revival of the dulcimer since we've had these "pick-ups" I call them, these electric pick-ups that are amplifiers and they give new life to this instrument. And when I play with five-string banjo and guitar, why, it makes pretty good music or at least folks all seem to enjoy it, and I

Lilly McGhee Ward Swick near Bidwell, Ohio, 1955.
Photo by James W. Grimes

Lilly McGhee Ward Swick and Ken Ward near
Bidwell, Ohio, 1955. Photo by James W. Grimes

guess that's the way to tell whether music is good or not and they can't keep their feet still.

We tape-recorded Ken Ward playing on his dulcimer the classic "Golden Slippers," and we also recorded the playing of his mother, Lilly McGhee Ward Swick, born in the area in 1882, who had been playing since she was a girl.

While Bob White played seated, both Ken and his mother preferred to play standing up. They liked to put the instrument on a table, note with a clothespin, and pluck either with a pick or a piece of wood or even a feather. Bob White seemed to use the words "dulcimer" and "dulcerine" interchangeably, but Ken and his mother knew the instrument only as "dulcerine."

Ken Ward made his first dulcimer in 1925, patterned after the one Mrs. Swick had owned since it was made for her in about 1895. Ken's dulcimer was very similar in design to Bob White's: both dulcimers had mechanical tuners and round sound-holes, laid out in triangular patterns.

I was interested to learn that Mrs. Swick's dulcimer (the model for Ken's) had been made for her by a "Butcher." The first dulcimer Bob White's father, Wilbur White, owned was made by Wilbur White's uncle, George Butcher. Bob White told us that Butcher had in turn modeled his dulcimer on still an earlier maker, John Wright

Charles Ralston with the author in Gallia County, Ohio, 1955.
Photo by James W. Grimes

of nearby Eno, Ohio. So John Wright may have been the earliest known maker in this tradition.

I was so excited by all this dulcimer lore that I had forgotten my usual inquiry for "old songs." But Ken asked if I'd like to hear an old lullaby his Grandmother Ward sang to him. So it was almost by accident that I collected Ken's version of "The Liar's Song," a song probably first sung in Elizabethan England.

Ken sang three verses of his grandmother's song that day, and later remembered another verse which he sent me in a letter, with the lines "a flea heave a tree / with a hammer in his knee." Ken also wrote about his paternal grandmother and the possible origins of the song. Her grandparents settled in Ohio after crossing Pennsylvania in their travels from Scotland. Ken wrote:

> Grandmother Ward was a Vance and her folks came from "across the sea." I'll tell you what she told me. They came in sailboats and it took six weeks. Big fish followed them and they were afraid they would upset the boat. They threw over food to get rid of them. They came from Scotland and that is probably where the "lying song" came from.

Ken Ward remained a good friend, and we enjoyed corresponding and seeing one another at festivals over the years. When he

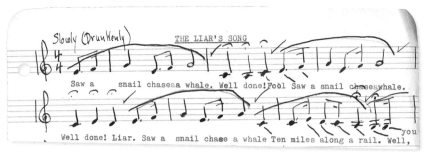
"The Liar's Song" as sung by Ken Ward. Notation by the author

visited me in Granville, I was pleased to meet his young daughter, Kendra, who has carried on her family's traditions with a very successful career as a folklorist and performer.

The last person we met on that day in March 1955—our "dulcimer day"—was Charles Ralston, one of those who knew of George Butcher and kept the tradition going in that area. An uncle and neighbor of Ken Ward, Ralston said his dulcimer was made out of an old bedpost.

The Liar's Song
Saw a snail chase a whale.
Well done, liar!
Saw a snail chase a whale.
Well done, fool!
Saw a snail chase a whale,
Ten miles on a rail.

Refrain:
You old bloody drunk, boys,
And I'm a jolly fool.

Saw a crow flying low.
Well done, liar!
Saw a crow flying low.
Well done, fool!
Saw a crow flying low,
Ten miles under snow.
Refrain

Saw a sow skimming milk.
Well done, liar!
Saw a sow skimming milk.
Well done, liar!
Saw a sow skimming milk,
And her pigs a'weaving silk.
Refrain

13 Arthur Byrd Fields

Christ in the Garden

BORN IN IRONTON in Lawrence County, Ohio, in 1888, Arthur Fields sang a beautifully condensed version of "Christ in the Garden," a solo religious or "white spiritual" survival from the early nineteenth century, when circuit-riding preachers taught hymns along with the gospel. Singing in worship was a tradition in many religious sects in the early decades of the state of Ohio, when tunes or "airs," borrowed from old ballads, were used locally for hymns printed without tunes in songsters and hymnals.

I met Arthur Fields through his nephew, Bill Fields, an Ohio State University graduate student in his thirties when he came to Ohio Folklore Society meetings in Columbus dragging his big guitar and singing old songs he learned off records. I said, "I expect you've got better family songs than that down there near Ironton." And eventually I got some nice ones from Bill for my tape collection, including the Child ballad "Our Goodman."

Bill took me to see his uncle, Arthur Fields, at his home in Portsmouth, some thirty miles from Ironton. I tape-recorded Uncle Arthur, as I also called him, singing several old hymns he learned from his father, Ezekiel Byrd Fields, born in 1842 in Lawrence County.

"He was a great man to read his Bible and sing hymns," said Uncle Arthur of his father, adding that the hymns were sung just at home for the family and no longer in church, although they had been sung in church earlier, "not in my day, but in his day."

Later I returned to Portsmouth to tape-record Uncle Arthur singing a fuller but less poignant version of "Christ in the Garden" after refreshing his memory from the family hymnbook, an 1854 edition of *The Sweet Songster, A Collection of the Most Popular and Approved Songs, Hymns, and Ballads,* which had the words but not the tune. But, somehow, the traditional compression of his first version seems more beautiful—especially as sung in Uncle Arthur's true, high, clear tenor, with "old-style" holds and ornamental quavers.

Another of the hymns Uncle Arthur sang was from the African American tradition, "Must I Be Carried to the Skies." He learned it as a youth when he and his cousin visited a church where "lining out"—the oral tradition in which the minister delivers the text and the congregation sings in response—was still practiced. Uncle Arthur told me he was surprised at how moved he was by this style of singing, which reminded him of his father's singing of the old hymns.

Christ in the Garden

While passing a garden,
I paused there to hear
A voice of the stranger;
The planter was near.
I wept to behold Him;
I asked Him his name,
And He answered, "'Tis Jesus,
From Heaven I came."

"I am thy Redeemer;
For thee I must die.
The cup is most bitter,
But cannot pass by."
His eyes, bright as diamonds,
To Heaven was raised,
While the angels stood wondering
Around Him, amazed.

Ella Strawser Flack in Columbus, Ohio, mid-1950s. Photo by James W. Grimes. Anne Grimes Collection, American Folklife Center, Library of Congress

14 Ella Strawser Flack

Pretty Nancy • Barb'ry Allen

ROSS COUNTY

ELLIE FLACK OF Columbus was a sure singer in the "old style" of early British ballads, handed down in her Ross County, Ohio, family. Ellie shared this tradition with her younger cousin, Bessie Weinrich, another important contributor, who still lived in Ross County. Ellie and Bessie were delightful ladies—charming and witty, respected and beloved in their communities, in which both had lovely, heirloom-filled homes.

Born in Londonderry, Ohio, in 1877, Ellie learned many of her songs from her mother, Abbie Strawser, and her grandmother, Betsy Dixon Boblett (Bessie's great-great-aunt), who came to Ross County as a young girl from "old Virginia." Ellie recalled going with her mother to feasts at the family homestead near Salt Creek.

> Then we'd all go into the living room and they'd sing and play—play old-fashioned organ, and my mother would play

the violin and they'd sing songs of all descriptions and they'd dance and have a swell time all afternoon.

Ellie was very cute—just a little flirt. At one memorable singing gathering in my home, she sang a lovely ballad, "Pretty Nancy," she said her husband liked to hear her sing when the couple was courting.

Though ballads like "Pretty Nancy" often tell of lords and ladies, they are not always associated with Britain but rather with local happenings. I've been told, for instance, that the subject of one of the best-known Child ballads, "Barbara Allen," lived in several certain places in Ohio, and even "Bold Robert" (or Robin Hood) has been thought of as a local hero.

Ellie's version of "Barbara Allen" had a fine tune and a full text. She sang it in an old style of singing.

Pretty Nancy

Come all you unmarried men. Come sit you down by me.
A bachelor's warning then come take by me.
When you court a pretty fair maid, don't court her too slow.
Nor don't court no other 'til she tells you no.

I courted pretty Nancy 'til her favors I won.
Straightway to another a'courting I run.
With the chief of my practice and the great of my woe
I lost pretty Nancy by courting too slow.

I wrote her a letter just for to let her know
That I had not forgot her although I didn't go.
But she wrote me an answer that I was too slow.
She was lawfully married before I did go.

The pain it struck William, it struck him for death,
Saying, "Must I die lovesick and never get well?"
Pretty Nancy came to hear this; it filled her with grief.
Saying, "I'll go to William and grant him relief."

"Oh, here stands a woman all by my bedside,
Which once might have been my lawfully bride.
But she wrote me an answer and I'll die for her sake."
She threw her arms around him and felt his heart break.

Since William has died in such pitiful mourn,
Let none but pretty Nancy to make her last mourn.
But since he died lovesick, I hope he's at rest.
Pretty Nancy, she fainted and died on his breast.

"Pretty Nancy" as sung by Ella Strawser Flack. Notation by the author

Barb'ry Allen (Child #84)
It was on the eighteenth day of May
When the small buds they were swelling.
Young Jimmie Grew on his deathbed he lay
For the love of Barb'ry Allen.

He sent a servant unto the town
To the place where she was dwelling.
And all she said when she got there,
"Young man I think you're a'dying."

Slowly, slowly, she got up,
And slowly she went to him.
And all she said when she got there,
"Young man, I think you're a'dying."

She had not got far out of the town
'Til she heard the church bells ringing.
"Sit down! Sit down these cold clay corpse
And let me look upon them."

They buried him in the churchyard,
And they buried her by the side of him.
Over him they grew a red, rosy bush,
And her they grew a briar.

They grew as high as a churchyard
'Til they could not grow no higher.
And there they entwined in a true lover's knot,
The red rose and the briar.

Let's See, 250 Divided By Four Is . . .

More than 250 years of folk singing experience was brought together in this quartet at the spring meeting of the Ohio Folklore Society. Mrs. Ella Flack, seated, admits to being a "year or two past ninety" while the other girls say only they're over 21. From the left they are, Mrs. Blanche Fullen, Mrs. Bessie Growden and Mrs. Faye Wemmer. (Photo by Lloyd Flowers.)

Folklore Group Gets Together

String Pickers Meet For Old-Time Singin'

Ol' Elvis would have withered | dropped the beat, no one seemed
in agony at the antics of a bunch | to seriously mind.
| Come to think of it, Elvis prob-

Blanche Fullen, Bessie Growden, Faye Wemmer, and Ella Flack on guitar at the Spring 1959 meeting of the Ohio Folklore Society in Columbus. Photo by Lloyd Flowers/Columbus Citizen

15 Blanche Wilson Fullen

The Cruel Mother • The Jolly Scotch Robbers

LAWRENCE
COUNTY

I SANG AT A father-daughter banquet in Columbus—mostly girls and their fathers—but still I put out my usual plea for songs, perhaps something a grandmother sang. There was one lady present, and she came up to say her mother sang an old song—something to do with "down by the greenwood side–ee-o."

I just caught my breath! I knew right away it was the Child ballad "The Cruel Mother." I said, "Does it have a terrible plot to it and awful things happen?"

The woman turned out to be the daughter of Blanche Wilson Fullen, who not only knew "The Cruel Mother" but could sing it in fifteen full verses with a complete plot and fine tune. Blanche or "Petey," as she was known to her family and friends, learned the song from her mother, Effie Levacy Wilson, who was born during the Civil War. Of Welsh-English ancestry, Effie Wilson sang "The Cruel Mother" to her children as a lullaby.

"She used to sing us to sleep with it, that terrible song," Petey said.

Born in the Ohio River town of Ironton in Lawrence County in 1887, Petey had been a stage singer who specialized in Irish dialect songs, but had never sung her family songs professionally. In fact, it was news to her that anyone outside her family knew them.

Petey invested in diamonds, and, after retiring from the stage, began to buy real estate and became an antiques dealer. When I met her she was a wealthy grandmother—and still a good-looking woman at age seventy—who lived in one of the finest houses in Upper Arlington, the suburb of Columbus where I also happened to live.

Another of her family songs, "The Jolly Scotch Robbers," came from her father, Joseph Kelsey Wilson, who was of Scots and Irish descent. A rare version of an early sixteenth-century ballad about a sea battle, it is an offshoot of the better-known "Henry Martin." Actually, Petey's version seems to be an unusual combination of three Child ballads: "Sir Andrew Barton" (Child #167), "Henry Martyn" (Child #250), and "Captain Ward and the Rainbow" (Child #287)—all having to do with seamen turned pirates.

Petey's father sang this old and dramatic ballad to her as a lullaby. She said she always anticipated his slow declamation of the final verse, in which Andrew Brattan tells the English sea captain, "Go home! Go home, you cowardly dog."

When I told her that in some versions it is Andrew Brattan who gets killed, she objected: "Oh, no, he had to be the triumphing hero; he has the best lines!"

The Cruel Mother (Child #20)

There was a maiden who lived in Cork,
All alone in the lie-lee-oh,
And she fell in love with her father's clerk.
Down by the greenwood side-ee-oh.

She courted him for a year and a day.
All alone in the lie-lee-oh,
At length her belly did her betray.
Down by the greenwood side-ee-oh.

She leaned her back against an oak,
All alone in the lie-lee-oh,
And first it bent and then it broke.
Down by the greenwood side-ee-oh.

She leaned her back against a thorn,
All alone in the lie-lee-oh,
And there two little babes were born.
Down by the greenwood side-ee-oh.

She took her garter from her knee,
All alone in the lie-lee-oh,
And she hung those babes up to a tree.
Down by the greenwood side-ee-oh.

She drew her penknife from her side,
All alone in the lie-lee-oh,
And she took the lives of those two babes.
Down by the greenwood side-ee-oh.

She went to the river to wash her hands,
All alone in the lie-lee-oh,
And the more she washed the deeper the stain.
Down by the greenwood side-ee-oh.

She dug a grave both wide and deep,
All alone in the lie-lee-oh,
And laid those two babes down to sleep.
Down by the greenwood side-ee-oh.

She covered them with a marble stone,
All alone in the lie-lee-oh,
And hoped her crime would not be known.
Down by the greenwood side-ee-oh.

Sitting sad and alone in her father's hall,
All alone in the lie-lee-oh,
She spied those babes a'playing ball.
Down by the greenwood side-ee-oh.

"Oh, babes, oh babes, if you were mine,"
All alone in the lie-lee-oh,
"I'd dress you up in silks so fine."
Down by the greenwood side-ee-oh.

"Oh, mother, oh mother, when we were yours,"
All alone in the lie-lee-oh,
"You neither loved us coarse nor fine."
Down by the greenwood side-ee-oh.

"Oh, babes, oh babes, come tell to me,"
All alone in the lie-lee-oh,
"What my portion is to be."
Down by the greenwood side-ee-oh.

"Oh, mother, oh mother, 'tis hard to tell."
All alone in the lie-lee-oh,
"You neither allowed us poor nor well."
Down by the greenwood side-ee-oh.

"Seven long years you'll rest in prison,"
All alone in the lie-lee-oh,
"And the rest of the time you'll roast in Hell."
Down by the greenwood side-ee-oh.

The Jolly Scotch Robbers

Oh, there were three brothers from Old Scotland,
Three robbers, three robbers were they,
And they all cast lot to see who would go
Out roving all o'er the salt sea.

Oh, the lot fell on to Andrew Brattan:
The youngest of the three,
That he should go roving all o'er the salt sea
Maintainments for the three.

Well, he had not sailed more than one summer's day,
Until a gay ship he did spy.
She was sailing far off, she was sailing far on,
And at length she came sailing close by.

"Who's there? Who's there?" cried Andrew Brattan.
"Who's there that sail her so nice?"
"It is a rich merchant chief from Old England.
Won't you please to let us pass by?"

"Oh no! Oh no!" cried Andrew Brattan,
"That thing it shall never be.
 Your ship we will capture; your gold take away,
 And your merry men drown in the sea."

 Well, the news went home to Old England,
 King George, he wore the crown,
 That his ship had been captured; his gold took away,
 And his merry men drowned in the sea.

"Go build me a ship," cried Captain Charles Stone,
"And build her both wide and sure.
 And I will bring in this Andrew Brattan
 Or my life no more will endure."

 Well he had not sailed more than one winter's day,
 Until a gay ship he did spy.
 She was sailing far off, she was sailing far on,
 And at length she came sailing close by.

"Who's there? Who's there?" cried Captain Charles Stone.
"Who's there that sail her so nice?"
"It's the Jolly Scotch Robbers from Old Scotland.
 Will you please to let us pass by?"

"Oh no! Oh no!" cried Captain Charles Stone,
"That thing it will never be.
 Your ship we will capture; your gold take away,
 And your merry men drown in the sea."

"Fight on! Fight on!" cried Andrew Brattan,
"Your threats I don't value a pin.
 And if you can show me bright brass without,
 I'll show you bright steel within."

 Oh then, oh then the battle began,
 And loudly the cannons did roar.
 And they had not fought more than an hour and a half,
 When Captain Charles Stone gave o'er.

"Go home! Go home, you cowardly dog,
 And tell your king for me
 That he can reign king all over dry land,
 But Andrew Brattan on the sea!"

Bob and Rose Gibson, early 1950s. Photo courtesy of the Bob Gibson Legacy Project, www.bobgibsonlegacy.com

16 Bob Gibson

Our Goodman

BOB GIBSON, THE popular folksinger and marvelous banjo player, came to a party at my house after an Ohio Folklore Society meeting and ended up staying the night—sleeping in the basement!

This was in the early 1950s, and Bob was attending the folklore meeting as part of his early quest for good songs, before he became known to a wider audience. He was just getting started in his career and living in Cleveland with his wife, Rose.

Bob visited us several times, and I visited the Gibsons in Chicago, where we saw Bob perform at the Gate of Horn. Bob and I exchanged material, including through tape-recording. I taped his singing, and I also gave him a tape of my singing of traditional songs that I had collected. Later, we kept in touch through cards and letters. The Gibsons also visited my friend and mentor Mary O. Eddy at her home in Perrysville, Ohio. Her book *Ballads and Songs from Ohio* was much admired by Bob.

Bob and Rose Gibson, early 1950s. Photo courtesy of the Bob Gibson Legacy Project, www.bobgibsonlegacy.com

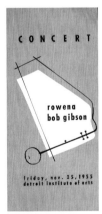

Rowena/Bob Gibson concert program cover designed by Bill Reik. Reproduced by permission from Constance Reik

During one session at our house, Bob sang a version of "Our Goodman," a Child ballad that I collected from several people in Ohio, including Arthur Fields's nephew, Bill Fields, in Ironton. Bob also contributed that day several other bawdy songs that though not of the Ohio tradition added to my research into this genre.

Another time, I joined Bob in singing "Run Come See" or "Wreck of the Pretoria," a Bahamian song that memorializes a great hurricane that struck Andros Island in 1929. Bob also recorded what he referred to as "The Bob Gibson Five-Minute Banjo Course," in which he credits Pete Seeger for the suggestion on getting the rhythm right in the basic strum (Think: "Chat–ta–noo–ga"). He ended the lesson by playing "Hard Ain't It Hard."

Around 1957, Bob talked about wanting to do an album of his singing some of the traditional songs that I had collected, with my writing the liner notes. Somehow that project never got done, and I lost touch with the Gibsons after the early 1960s.

Our Goodman (Child #274)

Last night as I come home, drunk as I could be,
Found another mule in the stable, where my mule oughta be.
"Come here honey, baby, explain yourself to me.
How come another mule in the stable, where my mule oughta be?"
"Now crazy, now silly, can't you plainly see?
There's nothin' but a milk cow that my grandma gave to me."
Travelled this wide world over, a million times or more,
A saddle on a milk cow, I've never seen before.

Other night when I come home, drunk as I could be,
I found another coat on the coat rack, where my coat oughta be.
"Honey, baby, explain yourself to me.
How come another coat on the coat rack, where my coat oughta be?"
"Honey, oh silly, can't you plainly see?
There's nothin' but a bed quilt, that your grandma sent to me."
I've travelled this world over, a million times or more,
Pockets on a bed quilt, I've never seen before.

Other night when I come home, drunk as I could be,
I seen another head on the pillow where my head oughta be.
Said "Honey, baby, explain this thing to me.
How come another head on the pillow, where my head oughta be?"
"Honey, sugar baby, can't you plainly see?
There's nothin' but a cabbage head, that my grandma give to me."
I've travelled this world over, a million times or more,
A hat on a cabbage head, I've never seen before.

A. B. Graham in Columbus, Ohio, 1957. Photo by Mac Shaffer courtesy of the Columbus Dispatch

17 **A. B. Graham**

Hayes Campaign Song • *Yankee Doodle*

A FOUNDER OF the 4-H Club program, Albert B. Graham was a pioneer educator who had a tremendous impact not only on Ohio schools but on education throughout the nation.

In May 1957 Mr. Graham was senior guest at a party for "my" singers of traditional songs and dulcimer players—twenty in all, just from Franklin County. I taped forty-one items during the festivities, many of which I had previously collected individually, but some "new" ones were recalled in the group situation. We never had a better party at our house—it was really out of this world!

A. B. Graham became one of "my" contributors when we taped items like his "Hayes Campaign Song" that he remembered sung as a boy in his hometown of Lena, Champaign County, Ohio, during the 1876 presidential campaign between Republican Rutherford B. Hayes and Democrat Samuel J. Tilden. Although he was only about eight years old at the time, Mr. Graham remembered a "pretty sharp" campaign, as he said before taping his song:

> There was a good deal of rivalry and close voting, and when it was all done it had to be thrown into an election committee, made up of five members of the House, Senate, and five from the Supreme Court. And it was decided 8 to 7 in favor of Hayes. . . . Noisy politicians made some statements that

stirred up people a little bit. Us children in our community we pretty near shed some tears over some of the imaginative realities of the thing.

Graham learned many of his songs from his father, Joseph A. Graham, who had been active in the "old-time singing schools" and enjoyed teaching the songs to young Albert and his younger sister, Lettie.

"Once in a while he would throw in a little 'tricky' one," Graham said of his father. Graham then began playing "Yankee Doodle" by tapping the top of his head or pate while changing the pitch with his throat.

One of his father's old songs, "Three Jolly Welshmen," had been passed down through the generations, probably going back to Scotland. A. B. Graham's great-grandfather came from Scotland and settled in Bucks County, Pennsylvania, and his son (Graham's grandfather) moved to western Champaign County, Ohio, in 1834, having disagreed with his father's idea that a steel plow would poison the soil.

A. B. Graham became friends with a fellow "senior" contributor and Ohio Folklore Society member, John Bodiker, whose life had differed from Graham's in many respects but who shared with him the experience of being raised on a farm and then losing the farm at a young age after the death of his father—in Graham's case when he was just eleven years old.

At Bodiker's request, Graham sent him a long letter about his life and career. His description of boyhood chores on the farm said in part, "This was all to the good for it established the worthwhileness of honest labor; it dignified farm work. However, I never forgot [the] opportunity at milking time to squirt milk at a cat's mouth."

At ninety years of age, A. B. Graham rarely missed a meeting of the Ohio Folklore Society, where he told stories and sang songs as well as demonstrating string and paper tricks. Dear and wise, Mr. Graham was wonderful, too, with young people. My daughter Mindy remembers sitting on his lap, learning several string tricks and listening to his tricky "Yankee Doodle."

Hayes Campaign Song

Old Sam, you haven't got a man.
Old Sam, you haven't got a man.
Old Sam, you haven't got a man
That wouldn't follow old Hayes's band.

Better pay your taxes early in the morning.
Better pay your taxes early in the day.
Better pay your taxes early in the morning,
And follow old Hayes's band.

Brodie Franklin Halley on his homestead in Gallia County, Ohio.
Photo courtesy of Michael D. Halley

18 Brodie Franklin Halley

Watermelon Smiling on the Vine • There's a Beautiful Home

GALLIA
COUNTY

THE BEST TRADITIONAL dulcimer player known to me was Brodie Halley of Mercerville, Gallia County, Ohio. His playing was outstanding, especially for its syncopated rhythms, which were done with a practiced combination of noting with a stick and clever finger pickings, strummings, and brushings.

Halley played on a dulcimer he bought in 1909 from a Civil War veteran—with sound holes of hearts, spades, diamonds, and clubs! He usually strummed with two fingers brushing back and forth in a style he learned from an uncle, Harvey Halley, who got his first dulcimer as a gift from his father in 1885.

Brodie Franklin Halley sent this photo of himself, taken in the early 1950s, to the author in 1957. Reproduced by permission from Michael D. Halley

I noticed sometimes Halley would lift his noter—instead of just sliding, he'd slide and lift. I asked him why he did that.

"I don't know. It just comes handy," he said.

A widower, Brodie Halley was seventy-four years old and living alone on the family homestead outside Gallipolis near the Ohio River when I met him in 1954. I was delighted not only by his singing and playing but by the beauty of his immaculately clean and well-preserved two-story log cabin. My lead to Brodie was Jason Sheppard of Gallipolis, a song contributor who helped me search for dulcimers.

For many years Brodie played dulcimer with a group of musicians for parties in Gallia County. The young people brought songbooks and sang, but did not dance.

"They'd make ice cream and eat sandwiches and play and sing," Brodie said, adding that the fiddler would start a song and then Brodie would come in on the dulcimer, playing the tune.

In addition to dulcimer instrumentals like "Watermelon Smiling on the Vine," "Goodbye Melinda," and "Birdie," Brodie sang and played an old hymn, "There's a Beautiful Home." He also sang unaccompanied a complete version of the ballad "Young Charlottie," which he remembered hearing as a boy.

I tried to get Brodie to come and play at the jamboree that followed the first public exhibit of my dulcimer collection in 1955 at the Ohio Historical Museum in Columbus, and invited him to send a photograph of himself to be featured with the other players and dulcimers. Unfortunately, he was unable to attend because of illness. In a letter to me in 1957, Brodie did send his picture, the photograph shown here (page 78).

There's a Beautiful Home

There's a beautiful home, far over the sea,
That beautiful place, for you and for me.
Beautiful home, so wonderfully fair,
That the Savior for me has gone to prepare.

Beautiful home, a crown I shall wear.
A golden white throne, forever we share,
United we'll be, with Jesus our King,
While the angels all o'er, His praises will sing.

Beautiful home, far over the sea,
That beautiful place, for you and for me.
That beautiful home, the sun outshine,
That heavenly home, someday to be mine.

A beautiful home, with friends I shall meet,
You're waiting for me, my coming to greet,
United we'll be, with Jesus our King,
While the angels all o'er, His praises will sing.

Beautiful home, far over the sea,
That beautiful place, for you and for me,
A beautiful home, the sun outshine,
That heavenly home someday will be mine.

Perry Harper in Ray, Ohio, 1955. Photo by James W. Grimes

19 Perry Harper

The Nightingale • House Carpenter • Dandoo

JACKSON
COUNTY

How I FOUND Perry Harper is significant in that it shows the way I found contributors. The lead came through an Ohio Wesleyan classmate, Mary Allen, who lived with her husband, Bill, and daughter, Jane, in an interesting old house, spacious and with ancient-treed surroundings, on historic Route 50 in the country across the Scioto River from Chillicothe, Ohio's first capital.

I often stayed with the Allens overnight. Both their families were Ross County settlers' descendants—of which they were very proud. The family also continued the tradition of being active leaders in many community, historic, agricultural, and patriotic organizations.

So, they were able and kind enough to get me booked for these groups' events, including programs at their home—perfect for outdoor folk music programs.

Through these stays and programs I became acquainted with a teenager who mowed their lawn, after he shyly told Mary that his grandfather sang songs like I did. That is what led me to Perry Harper.

Perry Harper was a wonderful true ballad singer: indeed, a rare and objective story-singing balladeer. We recorded Harper in his home in Ray, Ohio, which was settled in the early nineteenth century and where Harper's family had lived for several generations. Ray is literally a crossroads with one store and a few residences and barns in the lush farming area of northern Jackson County.

Harper sang from memory, with his eyes closed, rocking to the sure rhythm of his clear, high voice. After every piece he sang, he paused to use the spittoon at his feet. His songs included Child ballads he had learned from his father—"House Carpenter," "Barbara Allen," and a variant of "The Wife Wrapt in Wether Skin," which he called "Dandoo."

My major find from Perry Harper was "The Nightingale," or as he called it from its first line, "One Morning in May." This song he learned from an "old vet"—meaning a Civil War veteran. It is a centuries-old British soldier's song especially interesting since Harper's version has American additions: "Philadelphie" and "Chatanoogie."

Harper was an interesting character. Noted in the neighborhood as a singer, he was a blacksmith who also ran a gristmill. However, his professional fame was more widespread as a dog and horse trainer—as I learned from others including a sheep-herder at the Ohio State Fair in Columbus after I sang Harper's "Nightingale" there and mentioned his name.

The Nightingale

One morning, one morning, one morning in May,
I spied a fair couple a'making their way.
One was a gay lady, with her voice sweet and clear.
The other was a soldier, a bold volunteer.

"Oh, where are you going, my pretty fair maid?
Oh, where are you going," I say.
"I'm a'going to Chatanoogie on the banks of Lowlin,
To see the deep water glide and hear the nightingale sing."

We hadn't been there but a moment or two,
'Til out of his knapsack a fiddle he drew.
He played us one tune; made the valleys all ring,
"Hark, Hark, love listen, at the nightingale sing."

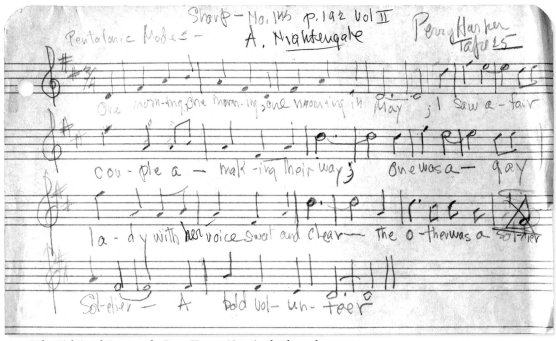

"The Nightingale" as sung by Perry Harper. Notation by the author

"Oh, now," said the lady, "would you marry, marry me?"
"Oh, no," said the soldier, "that never can be.
"Have a wife in Philadelphie and children twice three.
Two more in the army; too many for me."

Come all ye pretty fair maids and warning take by me.
Never place your affections on a soldier too free.
For they'll go off and leave you to fret and to mourn.
I am a poor strange girl and far from my home.

House Carpenter (Child #243)
"Well, met, well met, my own true love.
 Well met, well met," said he.
"I just sailed over the salt sea,
 Was all for the love of thee."

"I could have married a king's daughter fair,
 I'm sure she would have me.
 But I forsook her silver and gold,
 Was all for the love of thee."

"If you could've married a king's daughter fair,
 I'm sure you was to blame.
 For I have married a house carpenter,
 And I think him a nice young man."

"If you forsake your house carpenter
And go along with me,
I'll take you where the grass grows green,
On the banks of the Sit-a-ly."

She called her babe up to her knee.
She gave it kisses three,
Saying, "Stay at home, my sweet little babe.
Keep your father company."

They hadn't been on board two weeks.
I'm sure it was not three.
'Til this fair maid began for to weep,
And she wept most bitterly.

"Oh what are you weeping for, my gold?" said I,
"Oh, it's are you weeping for my store?
Oh, it's are you weeping for that house carpenter,
The one you shall see no more?"

"No, I'm not weeping for your gold," said I,
"No, I'm not weeping for your store.
But, oh, I'm weeping for that sweet little babe,
The one I shall see no more."

She hadn't been on board three weeks.
I'm sure it was not four.
'Til this brave vessel sprang a leak,
And she sank for to rise no more.

Dandoo (The Wife Wrapt in Wether's Skin, Child #277)

There's a little old man, Dandoo.
There's a little old man, and he lived in the west,
And he had an old wife that's none of the best.

Refrain (repeat after each verse):
Singin' heerum deerum whacka doodle,
    digramma yum,
Come-a-class, come-a-cling-o.

There's a little old man, Dandoo.
There's a little old man; he went out to plow.
Next thing he said was,
    "Is my breakfast ready now?"

There's a little old man, Dandoo.
"There's a piece of cold bread upon
    the shelf," Dandoo.
"There's a piece of cold bread upon the shelf,
Don't eat it now, for I'll eat it myself."

There's a little old man, Dandoo.
There's a little old man; he went out
    to his wether*-pen
And he catched an old wether
    and hung it on the pen.
And out of his skin he jerked him.

He took a stick and made it go whickity whack,
And wrapped it around his old wife's back.

There's a little old man, Dandoo.
There's a little old man, he traveled
    fourteen mile in fifteen days.
Didn't he have an awful time a'getting away?

*wether: castrated male sheep

Amanda Styers Hook with the author in Glouster, Ohio, 1958. Photo by James W. Grimes

20 Amanda Styers Hook

Terrell

ATHENS
COUNTY

BY THE MID-TWENTIETH century, very few people could remember and sing the traditional British ballads "Young Collins," "Locks and Bolts," "Down in Some Low Valley," and "True Lover's Farewell," as could Amanda Styers Hook, of Glouster, Ohio. It was thrilling to find these ballads still alive in Ohio, and well sung by Mrs. Hook. She also sang interesting local songs like "Seven Beers with the Wrong Woman" (!) and a song that became a standard in my performance repertoire, "Terrell."

I was introduced to Amanda Hook in 1958 by our mutual friend, Faye Wemmer, when I performed at the annual Jacksonville Homecoming. I also rode in the parade with some raccoons . . . that was real folksy! After the parade, Mrs. Hook invited me to her home on the Hartleyville Road north of Glouster, not far from where she was born in the Burr Oak region of Athens County. Because she didn't have electricity, we later went to the Methodist Church in Jacksonville to record.

I tape-recorded Mrs. Hook singing seventeen songs, including the Child ballads "Young Collins" ("Lady Alice"), "Lord Lovel," "Barbara Allen," and "House Carpenter." Many of her songs she learned from her mother, Margaret, and her grandmother, Nancy Grimes (no relation), who died in 1920 at age 107.

Mrs. Hook loved to sing and was known in her community as a singer, mostly of religious songs, although she apologized to me that she could not sing as well as when younger, when she said she could sing longer and higher, and also yodel. Her husband, Neal, said with pride that they'd "listen to her all night." The Hooks raised fourteen children, who learned to sing her songs.

Mrs. Hook had written all of her songs down in what she called "ballot books." They were several large notebooks indexed with general types together: old ballads, hymns, funny songs, play-parties, etc. She also included in these notebooks songs learned more recently from neighbors, relations, hymnals, songsters, re-cords, and radio. However, she readily recalled and sang their tunes, and in most cases could sing the words from memory with-out following her written manuscript.

Of the many fine songs Amanda Hook sang, one of the best was "Terrell," a local murder ballad. It is a parody of "The Boston Bur-glar," which was also a midwestern favorite, whose prototype was "Botany Bay," an early nineteenth-century British broadside ballad about an Australian penal colony.

"Terrell" tells the story of Bill Terrell, from the crossroads town of Gore, Ohio, who was eighteen when convicted of the murder of three members of the Weldon Family in Hocking County in 1878. The event became widely known in local lore, and there was still speculation about the "Gorey deed" among audience members who spoke to me after I performed the song.

Once after performing "Terrell" in Hocking County, I was taken aside to be told that the grass never grew again where the Weldon family was felled. Complicating things, another murderer, Josiah Terrill, of Meigs County, was executed in 1887 in the Ohio State Penitentiary. Although Bill Terrell's having come from the town of Gore contributes to the theme of the ballad, in fact the name comes not from "blood" but from the triangular shape of the township: gusset or gore-shaped.

Terrell

Terrell was born near Gore, my boys,
A place you all know well.
Brought up by honest parents,
The truth to you I'll tell.
Brought up by honest parents,
And proved most tenderly,
'Til Terrell become a roving boy
Which proved dishonesty.

Terrell's character was taken,
And he was sent to jail.
His parents tried to free him,
But it was all a fail.
The judge he passed the sentence,
And quickly wrote them down.
Then Terrell was cast in the county jail
That stands in Logan town.

Terrell took a ride on the west-bound train
All on one summer's day.
And every station he passed by
He heard the people say,
"There goes that noted murderer
Bound down with armor strong
He killed the Weldon family;
He's bound for Columbus town."

When he arrived at Columbus,
Stood pleading at the gate.
He took a view all around him.
How I pitied his sad face!
The green hills and the meadows
No more to see for years.
While Terrell stood there with a broken heart,
His poor eyes filled with tears.

His dear old aged father
Stood pleading at the bars,
Likewise his dear old aged mother.
How she tore her old gray hairs.
She tore her old gray hairs, my boys,
'Til the tears came rolling down.
Saying, "Son, oh son, what have you done,
This prison you are bound?"

Come all you false-hearted people,
Take warning from me.
Never go a'courting
For spite or jealousy.
For, if you do, you'll surely rue
And someday be like me,
Be hammering hard in hash, my boys,
In the Ohio penitentiary.

Postboy Road in Tuscarawas County, Ohio, mid-1950s. Photo by James W. Grimes

21 Arthur Emerson Kieffer

John Funston

TUSCARAWAS
COUNTY

THE "JOHN FUNSTON" ballad is one of my favorites. It tells the story of a long-remembered Ohio murder of a postboy (mail carrier) named William Cartmell, along the road between Coshocton and Newcomerstown in Tuscarawas County.

In 1825—the year ground was broken for the Ohio Canal—John Funston, a young Coshocton farmer, heard that a wagon-road drover was coming through carrying a large sum of money. Funston planned to rob the drover, but by mistake killed Cartmell. Funston was hanged for the crime in nearby New Philadelphia in the only public execution ever conducted in Tuscarawas County. The location where the murder took place later became the village named Postboy, after the murdered youth.

My first "find" of this ballad came in 1953 when I met Art Kieffer, a blind street singer with a tin cup on his guitar, playing for the

Saturday afternoon crowd in the county seat town of Jackson, Ohio. He was a wonderful singer, and I found—after exchanging old songs—that he remembered "John Funston," as sung by his mother, his uncle, and their mother, Grandmother McDabe, who was born in Mason County, West Virginia, in 1835.

I arranged to meet Kieffer the following week in Lancaster, Ohio, where we had a taping session in the back room of the Fairfield National Bank. He sang a number of songs that day, including a fragment of "John Funston" with a lovely tune.

Mary O. Eddy was the first in Ohio to collect "John Funston," and her two versions stick pretty close to historical fact and to accounts in the newspapers at the time. From the time I encountered "John Funston" in Eddy's collection, I was interested in both the facts and the lore surrounding the postboy murder and its song. There was much conjecture about it all, beginning with the newspaper accounts in which the name of the postboy was reported variously as "Cartmill" or "Cartwell." The name varies, too, in the ballads: Kieffer had it as "Courtland."

So when Art Kieffer called me up a few months after we had recorded in Lancaster to say that a visit with his mother had helped refresh his memory on "John Funston," Jimmie and I drove down to Kieffer's home in Ravenswood, West Virginia, on the Ohio River, to record him. His mother had taught him the rest of the song, and then checked him on it several times. "That's the full amount of it. . . . I feel certain that I have it all now," he told us.

The next year when I sang Kieffer's "Funston" in a church in Mt. Vernon, Ohio, a woman approached me after my program to say that she remembered her grandfather, S. E. Ferney, talking about the murder. Ferney lived in Columbus but grew up in New Philadelphia. I contacted Ferney, who told me that the murdered postboy had a living relative, Burleigh Cartmell. This was thrilling news to me.

Curiously, Burleigh Cartmell was an acquaintance of my parents through Ohio Wesleyan University, and I probably would have thought of the connection before, were it not for the variety of names I had encountered for the victim. I wrote to Burleigh Cartmell, who was then living in Delaware, Ohio.

Burleigh Cartmell wrote back that William Cartmell, the nineteen-year-old postboy, had been his great-uncle. Burleigh Cartmell in his letter recounted interesting details about the murder and the capture of Funston—including that William Cartmell was filling in that day for the regular postboy, who was ill. He said:

> The mother of Funston had told him that a wealthy drover would be coming through about that time and he laid in waiting. When he saw Cartmell riding alone he raised his rifle and shot him in the back.

Several years later, I decided to make a trip to the town of Post-boy. There I met Mrs. Ella Fenstermaker, who lived on a farm on Postboy Road. She told me about a poem that her father, A. C. Hursey, had written about the murder when he was editor of the *Newcomerstown Eye*, a newspaper founded in 1878 that became the *Newcomerstown Index* in 1882.

Mrs. Fenstermaker also introduced me to a friend, Frank Schlupp of Newcomerstown, who could sing a fragment of "John Funston," which I recorded. But, alas, I could find no one in the Postboy area who could actually sing the full ballad. Later, Mrs. Fenstermaker sent me the words of her father's poem, titled "A Song of 1825," which is similar in parts to the ballad as collected by Eddy.

Art Kieffer knew little of the origins of his family's version of the ballad except that it was probably originally from newspaper accounts. That his "John Funston" differs so choicely in detail from the other versions only adds to the lore and for my purposes is as vital as historical fact.

John Funston

As I come home, Dear Mother, I'll tell you what I see.
Tell you of a young man that hanged on a tree.
He was fair, neat, and handsome, light hair and blue eyes.
He wrought his own ruin by seeking a prize.

These words are as true words as ever has been told,
Funston a youth about twenty years old,
A fair-looking young man as ever you did see.
Yet he hanged by his neck from a black walnut tree.

He murdered William Courtland, a man of renown,
On the road that leads from Newport unto Coshocton town.
He murdered him; he robbed him of money and of goods.
And made his way home through a thicket of woods.

He went to Arizona; there he stayed about five years,
Came back to Ironton and thought that he'd be clear.
But the big sheriff found him at Jim Brooks's sale.
He gathered up that gentleman and laid him in jail.

On the second day of April, as they always had done,
They brought out John Funston; he confessed what he had done.
The jury found him guilty; the judge unto him said,
"You must hang by your neck, sir, until you are dead."

The doctor stood around him; his pulse he did feel,
Thinking the dead body of John Funston to steal.
Contrary to law and considered not right,
To steal the dead body of John Funston at night.

On the sixth day of April, one Friday afternoon,
They brought out John Funston and sang him a tune.
There were eight hundred people to witness the scene,
The hanging of John Funston, be he ever so mean.

His two little brothers brought a carriage that day
To haul the dead body of young Funston away.
Oh, when they got there, how they mourned, how they cried,
To think that on the gallows their brother had died.

They buried him in Brooklyn in the year of forty-nine.
They put him in a coffin of nice, yellow pine.
They sang and they played as they laid him away.
He only got justice the people all say.

His hopes for eternity must surely have been small.
He shed not a tear and he prayed not at all.
Oh, Father in Heaven, have mercy on Joe!
What becomes of a murderer, nobody does know.

Donald Langstaff with the author in his home, Toboso, Licking County, Ohio, 1954. Photo by James W. Grimes

22 Donald Langstaff

The Farmer's Curst Wife • Cottage Hill

LICKING
COUNTY

WHEN I SANG at the Ohio State Fair in Columbus in August 1953, I became acquainted with another performer, a fiddler named Frank Morrison, who invited me to chord on piano for his Licking County group that also included David V. Sidle on five-string banjo and his twenty-three-year-old son, Kenny, on fiddle. Kenny Sidle was to go on to become a master fiddler, winning many state and regional championships.

The next spring, Frank invited me to a gathering at the home of another friend and fiddle player, John Cromer, near Toboso, the eastern Licking County town where Kenny Sidle was born and where Morrison also had roots.

That's where I met Donald Langstaff, a fiddler who called himself "the Squirrel Hunter." He was marvelous. His version of "The

The author at the home of Donald Langstaff in Toboso, Licking County, Ohio, 1954. Photo by James W. Grimes

Donald Langstaff in his home, Toboso, Licking County, Ohio, 1954. Photo by James W. Grimes

Farmer's Curst Wife," a Child ballad, is exceptional. I found this song was known to many of my Ohio contributors, especially farmers. Langstaff sang it the same way my Grandmother Hagerman did, so his song seemed as familiar to me as "Mary Had a Little Lamb"—I mean, this is the way I'd always heard it.

But Langstaff's big contribution to my collection was a wonderful ballad called "Cottage Hill." He learned it from an uncle, Tom Langstaff, born in 1858 near Cottage Hill. Langstaff said of his uncle that he was the kind of person who whenever he heard a song never forgot it.

"I'm like that, too—you are, too, I'll bet," I said.

Cottage Hill was a tiny crossroads a few miles south of Toboso near where the Ohio Canal met the National Road. The boaters and drovers went to the tavern in Cottage Hill to drink and have a big time. But with the arrival of the trains, settlements like Cottage Hill along the canal and National Road changed or disappeared.

I thought "Cottage Hill" was a wonderful local ballad until Professor Tristram C. Coffin, the eminent Denison University folklorist who preceded me as secretary of the Ohio Folklore Society, pointed out that the same thing had been sung over in Pennsylvania about a big to-do over there! So that was fun.

I taped Langstaff singing several other songs as well as some group fiddle and banjo playing at Cromer's house that day.

Cottage Hill

Come all you good old rounders and a'listen to my rhymes.
Was on a Monday morning, the weather being fine,
I harnessed up my horses, my business to pursue,
And I went a'hauling wood as I always used to do.

But instead of hauling five loads I only hauled but four.
I got so drunk at Cottage Hill that I couldn't haul no more.
The saloon it was open; the whiskey was free.
When one glass was empty there's another 'n filled for me.

I met an old acquaintance; his name I dare not tell.
He was telling me that night where there was to be a ball.
I was hard to be persuaded but at last he did succeed.
I promised to meet him that night where the fiddle was to be.

I shouldered up my saddle and I marched out to the barn.
I saddled up old roan not thinking any harm.
I saddled up old roan and away I rode so still
That I hardly breathed aloud until I got to Cottage Hill.

My father followed after me, I often heard him say.
He must have had a partner or he could not have found the way.
He peeped in every crack where he thought there was a light
'Til his locks they were wet with the dews of the night.

And now then I'll tell you how our frolic did advance,
When four brave young fellas got on the floor to dance.
The music was willing and we all being strong
And we danced the "Bells of Ireland" for four straight hours along.

The morning sun had risen and we all had danced enough.
We spent a half an hour in a'raising cash for cuff.
We'll go home to our plows and we'll whistle and we'll sing.
And we never will be caught in such a scrape as this again.

Come all you good old people that is making such a fuss.
You've been guilty of the same and perhaps a whole lot worse.
Now when you go to tattle and tell the news about,
Don't tell the lie about it for it's bad enough without.

The Farmer's Curst Wife (Child #278)

There was an old woman lived under the hill *(whistle)*
But if she ain't dead, she's living there still.
To me high addle ding day addle ding die.

One wee little devil came up to the plow *(whistle)*
Saying, "One of your family I must have now."
To me high addle ding day addle ding die.

"It's not the youngest one that I crave *(whistle)*
But your old scolding wife; she I must have."
To me high addle ding day addle ding die.

He shouldered her up right over his back *(whistle)*
And like a bold peddler he waggled his pack.
To me high addle ding day addle ding die.

He carried her there and he bade her go in *(whistle)*
He bade her go in like an old scolding pin.
To me high addle ding day addle ding die.

Four little devils were baking some beans *(whistle)*
She up with a club and knocked out their brains.
To me high addle ding day addle ding die.

Two more little devils looked over the wall *(whistle)*
Saying, "Take her away or she'll murder us all."
To me high addle ding day addle ding die.

Three years have gone by ere this old woman came back *(whistle)*
She called for the mush she'd left in her pot.
To me high addle ding day addle ding die.

When she got home, her old man was in bed *(whistle)*
She up with a pewter pot; battered his head.
To me high addle ding day addle ding die.

What we'll do with this old woman I hardly can tell *(whistle)*
They won't have her in heaven; can't keep her in hell.
To me high addle ding day addle ding die.

Fanny Hagerman Laylin, the author's mother, in Columbus, Ohio, mid-1950s. Photo courtesy of the Grimes family

23 **Fanny Hagerman Laylin**

Froggie Went A'Courting • *Hush, My Babe*
There Was a Little Man • *God Moves in a Mysterious Way*
Father Grumble

RICHLAND
COUNTY

I WAS HOSTING a musical program on WOSU radio in Columbus in the 1940s when a scheduled guest called in sick at the last moment and, to fill the time, I sang some of my grandmother's songs. The response was tremendous, with listeners calling in similar passed-down family and community songs. That was the beginning of my folk music collection, and it came to include on tape some of my own grandmother's songs as sung by my mother, Fanny Hagerman Laylin.

The songs my mother sang to me as a child in Columbus, Ohio, represent a rich tradition of singing from Richland County, Ohio,

Adeline Hughes Hagerman, the author's grandmother, born in Richland County, Ohio, in 1856.
Photo courtesy of the Grimes family

where she was born into an Ohio pioneer family in 1884. Many of these songs—like "Froggie Went A'Courting," the lullaby "Hush, My Babe," and "There Was a Little Man," a nursery song that was sung, as Mother said, "with great gestures and hugging of children"—were traditional in many midwestern homes, not just my own.

My maternal grandmother, Adeline Palmer Hughes Hagerman, described very well this kind of traditional singing when she wrote in her later years about growing up in a family of six children on a farm near Mansfield in Weller Township in Richland County:

> One of the finest memories I have is of our singing. Everyone sang. . . . We sang about our work indoors and outdoors. At any time and in all seasons when out-of-doors, one could hear a boy as he was plowing, harrowing, cultivating, husking, or hoeing.
>
> We sang about our work in the kitchen, in the sitting room in the afternoon as we sewed, and in the winter evenings.
>
> It was not planned singing—oh, no. Someone would unconsciously hum a tune, another in the same unconscious manner would add bass or alto, and before the end of the verse there would be a full quartette. Usually everyone was busy at some work. Even those reading would hum a part without realizing he was singing.

Grandmother Hagerman grew up to marry Edward Hagerman, a young man from a neighboring family also descended from Richland County pioneers. Early in their marriage, he turned from farming to the ministry and became a well-known Methodist minister who for many years was an inspirational speaker on the Redpath Chautauqua lecture circuit. The Hagermans had four daughters, including my mother, Fanny.

From Granddaddy Hagerman, I learned "Methodist Pie," an echo of the Great Kentucky Revival of 1799 and the early 1800s that crossed the Ohio River. With the help of influential circuit-riding preachers, the spiritual revival left a mark on pioneer worship. The worship included camp meetings, where, in addition to "hellfire and damnation" preaching and hymn singing, a good time was had by all. Granddaddy Hagerman shared the song with me in fun, although he actually did not approve of the excesses of the "camp meeting" Revival period reflected in this ditty.

Most of the family songs I learned as a child came from Grandmother Hagerman's family, descended from Joseph and Elizabeth Dickens Ward, who were Richland County settlers. Joseph Ward had been the manager of a large estate near Repton in Derbyshire, England, where his ancestors had lived since the 1300s. He also taught music in Repton and was organist and choir director of his village church. On arriving in Richland County, besides farming

Joseph Ward established singing schools. Grandmother Hagerman wrote of the Wards, who were her maternal great-grandparents: "Joseph and Elizabeth were cultured, intensely religious and interested in good music. There has never been a descendant of that couple who had no music in his soul."

The Wards arrived in Ohio in 1819 after a harrowing sea voyage from England. Family lore has it that on the Wards' trip across the Atlantic, a violent storm came and all on board, including many of the crew, believed the vessel would go down. Joseph Ward gathered the passengers and crew in the hold and conducted a service of worship and prayer for deliverance.

The hymn Ward selected, "God Moves in a Mysterious Way," has been sung in our family ever since. I recall glorious and spirited singing of "The Hymn," with its old English tune, at reunions in Richland County in the 1920s—and in perfect eight-part harmony! My father (bass) joined Mother (alto) and me (soprano) in singing "The Hymn" for my tape collection in 1953.

As a folklorist, I typically took the family tradition of singing "God Moves in a Mysterious Way" rather for granted. But I found that other scholars were intrigued by the old Handelian tune, never found in hymnals. When I sang it at a New York Folklore Society meeting in the mid-1950s, several authorities told me that the only other known use of the tune was in Primitive Southern churches. The lyrics are by the English poet and hymnodist William Cowper (1731–1800).

A lullaby my mother sang to me, "Hush, My Babe," was sometimes included in pioneer Christmas observances and may date from the early eighteenth century. The tune (widely recognized as that of the old favorite "Go Tell Aunt Rhodie") has been ascribed to the philosopher Jean-Jacques Rousseau, who was also a music copyist, and the words to the great hymnologist Isaac Watts, author of such enduring hymns as "O God, Our Help in Ages Past" and "Joy to the World."

I created a dulcimer accompaniment that I usually played when performing "Hush, My Babe," holding the instrument in the style I learned from Jane McNerlin, an important contributor of dulcimer playing and lore to my tape collection.

"There Was a Little Man," another of my mother's songs probably brought to Richland County by the Wards, ends with a funny "quack, quack, quack" drake call. The words were widely published in various versions in early collections of nursery rhymes, going back to the mid-1700s, and are probably even much older. One imaginative suggestion referenced in Opie's classic dictionary of nursery rhymes is that it depicts Sir Francis Drake.

My performances of Grandmother Hagerman's songs on WOSU radio led to my career as a folksinger and folklorist as I began performing traditional songs at schools, historical societies, and social clubs throughout Ohio. Especially in the early days, Mother sometimes came with me. One of Grandmother Hagerman's favorite songs was "Father Grumble," a song about a husband who traded jobs with his wife because he thought "he could do more work in one day than his wife could do in three." If I didn't include "Father Grumble" in my program, Mother would admonish me: "But you didn't sing your grandmother's song!"

Froggie Went A'Courting

Mr. Froggie went a'courting and he did ride. Uh-huh.
Froggie went a'courting and he did ride,
A sword and a pistol by his side. Uh-huh.

Rode up to Miss Mousey's door. Uh-huh.
Rode up to Miss Mousey's door,
Where he had been many times before. Uh-huh.

"Mistress Mouse, are you within? Uh-huh.
Mistress Mouse, are you within?"
"Yes, kind sir, I sit and spin." Uh-huh.

Took Miss Mousey on his knee. Uh-huh.
Took Miss Mousey on his knee,
And said, "Miss Mouse will you marry me?" Uh-huh.

"Without my uncle Rat's consent. Un-uh.
Without my uncle Rat's consent,
I would not marry the president." Uh-uh.

Uncle Rat laughed and shook his fat sides. Ho-ho.
Uncle Rat laughed and shook his fat sides,
To think his niece would be a bride. Uh-huh.

Where will the wedding supper be? Uh-huh.
Where will the wedding supper be?
Way down yonder in a sycamore tree. Uh-huh.

And what will the wedding supper be? Uh-huh.
What will the wedding supper be?
Roasted turkey and a buckeye bee. Uh-huh.

First come in was a bumble bee. Bzzz.
First come in was a bumble bee
With his fiddle on his knee. Bzzz.

Next come in was a trundle-bed bug. Uh-hm.
Next come in was a trundle-bed bug
With his whiskey and a rum-a-jug-jug. Uh-hm.

Last come in was an old black snake. Zip.
Last come in was an old black snake
With the custard and the cake. Uh-huh.

They all sat down for to have a chat. Uh-huh.
All sat down for to have a chat
When in walked in the kitten and the cat. Oh-oh.

Miss Mouse went flying up the wall. Uh-huh.
Miss Mouse went flying up the wall,
And there she had a great big fall. Uh-huh.

They all went flying 'cross the lake. Uh-huh.
They all went flying 'cross the lake
And there were swallowed by a big black snake.
    Uh-huh.

That was the end of one, two, three. Uh-huh.
That was the end of one, two, three:
The frog and the cat and Miss Mousey. Uh-huh.

There's bread and cheese upon the shelf.
    Uh-huh.
There's bread and cheese upon the shelf.
If you want any more, you can sing it yourself.
    Uh-huh.

Hush, My Babe

Hush, my babe, lie still and slumber;
Holy angels guard thy bed.
Heavenly blessings without number
Gently falling on thy head.
How much better thou are attended
Than the Son of God could be,
When from Heaven He descended
And became a child like thee.

Soft and easy is thy cradle;
Coarse and hard thy Savior lay
When His birthplace was a stable,
And His softest bed was hay.
Oh, to tell the wondrous story
How His foes abused their King,
How they killed the Prince of Glory
Makes me angry while I sing.

Hush, my babe, lie still and slumber.
Holy angels guard thy bed.

There Was a Little Man

There was a little man,
And he had a little gun,
And his bullets were made of lead, lead, lead.
He went to the brook
And he shot a little duck,
And he shot it through the head, head, head.
He shot it through the head.

Then he went home
To his old wife Joan
And bade her a good fire make, make, make,
For to roast the little duck
That he shot at the brook,
And he'd go and shoot the drake, drake, drake.
He'd go and shoot the drake.

He shot at the drake
But he missed his mark,
And the drake flew away
Crying, "Quack, quack, quack!"

God Moves in a Mysterious Way

God moves in a mysterious way
His wonders to perform.
He plants his footsteps in the sea
He plants his footsteps in the sea
And rides upon the storm
And rides upon the storm
And rides upon the storm.

Ye fearful saints fresh courage take
The clouds ye so much dread
Are big with mercy and will break
Are big with mercy and will break
With blessings on your head
With blessings on your head
With blessings on your head.

Judge not the Lord by feeble sense
But trust Him for His grace
Behind a frowning providence
Behind a frowning providence
He hides a smiling face
He hides a smiling face
He hides a smiling face.

Blind unbelief is sure to err
And scan His work in vain
God is His own interpreter
God is His own interpreter
And He will make it plain
And He will make it plain
And He will make it plain.

Father Grumble

There was an old man who lived in the woods,
As you can plainly see,
Who said he could do more work in one day
Than his wife could do in three.

"If this be true," the old woman said,
"Then you will allow
That you can mind the house one day
While I go drive the plow.

"But you must milk the tiny cow
For fear she will go dry,
And you must watch the little pigs
That are within the sty.

"And you must watch the speckled hen
For fear she lay astray,
And don't forget the reel of yarn
That I spun yesterday."

So the old woman took the reins in her hand
And went to drive the plow.
And the old man took the stool in his hand
And went to milk the cow.

And Tiny hitched and Tiny flinched.
Tiny cocked her nose.
And Tiny gave the old man such a kick
That the blood ran down his nose.

"It's Hey, my good cow, and Ho, my good cow,
And now, my good cow, stand still!
If I ever milk this cow again,
'Twill be against my will."

Then he milked the tiny cow
For fear she would go dry,
And then he watched the little pigs
That are within the sty.

And then he watched the speckled hen
For fear she'd lay astray.
But he forgot the reel of yarn
That his wife spun yesterday.

He vowed by all the stars in the sky
And all the birds in the tree
That his wife could do more work in one day
Than he could do in three.

He vowed by all the stars in the sky
And all the birds in Heaven
That his wife could do more work in one day
Than he could do in seven.

Broadside of "Sinclaire's Defeat" published by Frazer Ells Wilson in 1938. Reproduced by permission from Robert F. Wilson

24 Lottie Leas

St. Clair's Defeat

DARKE COUNTY

LOTTIE LEAS, A well-respected teacher of piano, was in her seventies when I came to call on her at her home in Greenville in Darke County in the west-central part of Ohio near the Indiana line. There she sang and told me about "St. Clair's Defeat" or "Sinclaire's Defeat," as it was known in her family. She had heard it sung by her mother, aunt, and grandmother, Anna Stephens Woods, who was born in Darke County in 1822.

A strong and wonderful old ballad, "St. Clair's Defeat" is one way that Ohio pioneers kept alive "the fearful and terrifying memory," as local Darke County historian Frazer E. Wilson put it to me, of one of the bloodiest battles of the "Indian Wars."

General Arthur St. Clair, a distinguished Revolutionary War general, was appointed by President George Washington to serve as governor of the Northwest Territories. In 1791 near the headwaters of the Wabash River, some one thousand under St. Clair's command were killed when they were ambushed by Miami Chief Little Turtle. Survivors, including St. Clair, fled to Fort Jefferson, which then stood south of Greenville.

"St. Clair's Defeat," a topical ballad circulated through broadside prints, is said to have hung on the walls of many homes during the early 1800s; but by the 1950s as a pioneer ballad it was nearly forgotten in Ohio. In 1951, my friend Bill Utter, a professor of history at Denison University, sent me his find of a printed broadside of the ballad published in 1938 by Frazer E. Wilson.

Wilson's broadside "Sinclaire's Defeat," printed with words and melody, notes that the song should be sung "with sad emotion." The words follow closely the details of the battle. However, in comparing the text to the list of officers participating, it is interesting to note that oral tradition has changed some of their names slightly. And it reflects that many of the soldiers were, like perhaps the balladmaker, veterans of the Revolution.

I contacted Wilson, who wrote to me how he came across the ballad. In the 1930s he was working on a book on St. Clair when he happened to mention something about his research in the presence of Lottie Leas' aunt, Anna Woods Turner. Born in Darke County in 1865 into a family described by Wilson as "remarkable" for its musical talent, Mrs. Turner sang the ballad in what he described as a very low voice, "sort of the crooning type, very limited in range, but rich in quality."

Intent on preserving the ballad, Wilson had Mrs. Turner sing it to her niece Lottie Leas. As a trained musician Miss Leas was able to notate the tune as well as write down the lyrics of the song. Miss Leas told me that she checked and re-checked the notation of the tune with both her aunt and her mother to make sure it was correct because—despite her musical training and abilities—Miss Leas herself did not inherit the singing ability that was in her family. She could not hold on to a tune!

Miss Leas was a good musician, however, and she knew what the real tune was. So, when I tape-recorded Miss Leas in the early 1950s, we repeated several times her singing of it to be sure that we had the tune that seemed right to her, as she heard it sung tradition-ally in her family.

The origin of the tune interested me. The earliest written record I could find of "St. Clair's Defeat" was in *Recollections* by Henry M. Brackenridge, published in 1834. Brackenridge told of hearing it around 1800 at a Pittsburgh racetrack being chanted in a tone "part nasal and part guttural" by a blind ballad-maker, Dennis Loughey. Nearby Loughey, Brackenridge said, a fiddler was "making the dust fly" while playing reels. So it may have been there that the ballad came to be sung to the fiddle tune. It is a tune still widely popular with fiddlers: "Bonaparte's Retreat."

In 1954, I performed "St. Clair's Defeat" in Chillicothe in Ross County in the south-central part of Ohio where a number of sur-vivors of the battle settled. A member of the audience, Mrs. Anna Barrett of a Chillicothe pioneer family, remembered her mother and aunt singing the ballad. From her, I got my last collected verse that refers to one of those killed on "November the fourth in the year of '91." General Richard Butler, the second in command to St. Clair, was a distinguished Revolutionary War general and a close friend of General "Mad" Anthony Wayne who arrived after the battle to bury the victims. My version of "St. Clair's Defeat" is from Lottie Leas but ends with the lyrics I collected from Anna Barrett:

Oh, sweet Dicky Butler, Wayne'll nae see you more.

A Miami did scalp you, and the ground ran with gore!

St. Clair's Defeat

'Twas November the fourth in the year of ninety-one,
We had a sore engagement near to Fort Jefferson.
Sinclaire was our commander, which may remembered be,
For there we left nine hundred men in the Western Territory.

At Bunker's Hill and Quebeck, where many a hero fell,
Likewise at Long Island (it is I the truth can tell).
But such a dreadful carnage may I never see again
As happened near Saint Mary's upon the river plain.

Our army was attacked just as the day did dawn,
And was soon overpowered and driven from the lawn.
They killed Major Oldham, Levin, and Briggs likewise,
While horrid yells of savages resounded through the skies.

Yet three hours more we fought them, 'til then we had to yield,
When nine hundred bloody warriors lay stretched upon the field.
Says Colonel Gibson to his men, "My boys, be not dismayed,
I am sure that true Virginians were never yet afraid.

"Ten thousand deaths I'd rather die than they should gain the field,"
With that, he got a fatal shot, which caused him to yield.
Says Major Clark, "My heroes, we can here no longer stand.
We'll strive to form in order and retreat the best we can."

The word "Retreat!" being passed around, there was a dismal cry.
Then helter-skelter through the woods like wolves and sheep they fly!
This well-appointed army, which but a day before
Had braved, defied all danger, was like a cloud passed o'er.

Alas, the dying and wounded (how dreadful was the thought!)
To the tomahawk and scalping knife in misery are brought.
Some had a thigh and some an arm broke on the field that day,
Who writhed in torment at the stake to close the dire affray.

To mention our brave officers, is what I wish to do.
No sons of Mars e'er fought more brave or with more courage true.
To Captain Bradford I belonged, to his artillery.
He fell that day amongst the slain—a valiant man was he.

Oh, sweet Dicky Butler, Wayne'll nae see you more.
A Miami did scalp you, and the ground ran with gore!

25 Bascom Lamar Lunsford

A Bonny Lass, a Happy Lass

BASCOM LAMAR LUNSFORD—the North Carolina ballad singer, folk expert, banjo picker, fiddler, and folk dance expert—was a marvelous guy. Among his many accomplishments, he was a folk music collector and folk festival founder who in 1928 began the first festival of authentic American folk music in his annual Mountain Dance and Folk Festival in Asheville, North Carolina.

Born in 1882 in Mars Hill, North Carolina, where his father was a college professor, Lunsford attended Rutherford College (now Duke University) and Trinity Law School. In addition to the practice of law and his many activities in folklore, he had been at various times an auctioneer, college instructor, politician, editor of a country newspaper, and World War I Department of Justice agent.

As a collector, Lunsford's repertoire of collected songs included some 350 items he sang in 1949 for the Library of Congress, the largest number ever recorded by a single performer. He also composed songs, including the popular "That Good Old Mountain Dew," and was a wonderful banjo player.

I met Lunsford when I performed in 1952 at his Asheville festival. Afterward, I enjoyed a gathering at his place on South Turkey Creek in Buncombe County along with other festival participants including ballad singer Virgil Sturgill and banjo players Harry West and Roger Sprung. That festival in Asheville also proved significant to me because I met Marcus Martin, the fiddler, which led me to his son, Wade, and my first purchase of a dulcimer. It was that summer near Asheville that I met Carl Sandburg.

Lunsford and I remained in touch, in part because of family visits to Asheville, where Jimmie grew up and his mother still lived. Lunsford was a guest at our house in 1958 when he was in Columbus at my invitation to lecture and perform at the Ohio Folklore Society's annual spring meeting at the Ohio Historical Museum.

It was during Lunsford's 1958 visit to Columbus that I taped his singing and playing of a bawdy song he called "A Bonny Lass, a Happy Lass" that he said he had learned from Paul Johns, "a good five-string banjo player," from Alleghany County, North Carolina. Lunsford said it was the first time he had recorded this song, explaining, "It happens to be a type of song that I have made no recording or written record of because it's the kind of thing we naturally remember pretty readily anyway."

Ticket to Bascom Lamar Lunsford's annual
Mountain Dance and Folk Festival in Asheville,
North Carolina, 1958.

A Bonny Lass, a Happy Lass

A bonny lass, a happy lass,
On one rainy day
I took my true love by the hand,
And led her far astray,
And led her far astray.

"I could cover you so close
 Should any chance to pass,
 They'd think it was a drunkard low,
 Snorin' in the grass,
 Snorin' in the grass."

"You could cover me again,
 If you was any man."
"Well, if I could I surely would,
 But baldy he won't stand,
 Baldy he won't stand."

I've often heard my Grandma say,
And she's a good old wife,
That any fair young maiden's head
Would bring the dead to life,
Would bring the dead to life.

If I should pass again this way,
And tears don't dim my eyes,
I'd call and see that pretty little girl,
Rollin' up her thighs,
A rollin' up her thighs.

W. E. Lunsford holding his father's dulcimer in Columbus, Ohio, mid-1950s. Photo by James W. Grimes.

26 W. E. Lunsford and the John H. Lunsford Dulcimer

Turkey in the Straw

LAWRENCE
COUNTY

W. E. "Eddie" Lunsford had a wide repertoire of songs, many of them traditional ones from his father, John H. Lunsford, a railroad man and cabinetmaker. In the 1870s he made for Eddie, who was just a little boy at the time, an exceptionally fine dulcimer with mother-of-pearl inserts on the fretboard and tuners. It also has rhinestone sets on the neck!

As a young man in the early 1890s, Eddie Lunsford played his dulcimer along with harmonica and drums as a "one-man band" professional entertainer in hotels in the Ohio River town of Ironton in Lawrence County. But when I met him in 1955 at an exhibit of my dulcimer collection at the Ohio Historical Museum in Columbus,

W. E. Lunsford with the author in Columbus, Ohio, mid-1950s. Photo
by James W. Grimes. Smithsonian Institution Collections, National
Museum of American History, Behring Center

he was a barber by trade. He had lived some fifty years in Columbus and was not playing his dulcimer. In fact, other than his own,
he hadn't seen or heard of dulcimers for years and was completely
surprised at the extent of the tradition, having thought the dulcimer
to be a Lawrence County local item. He pronounced and wrote the
word as "delsmer."

Eddie began playing his dulcimer again and became active in
the Ohio Folklore Society. Also an accomplished banjo picker and
guitar player, he contributed on dulcimer to my taped collection two
classic tunes, "Cindy" and "Turkey in the Straw."

We became friends, and Eddie gave me his father's handwritten "ballad book" and told me he had willed me his dulcimer. He
also made for me a lovely frame of intricate layered matchsticks that
holds my honorary life membership award from the Ohio Historical
Society. On the back of the frame is written: "From W. E. Lunsford,
the Delsmer Man."

When Eddie died in 1958, his family contacted me to let me
know that he had indeed willed me his dulcimer. However, they
said they just weren't ready yet to give it up. A couple of years later
when a flash flood brought water within inches of the instrument,
his widow, Alda, called me to come get it. She said Eddie had "spoken from the grave!"

The author holding her dulcimer made by Wade Martin.
Photographer unknown

27 Marcus and Wade Martin and the Martin Dulcimers

THE FIRST DULCIMER I owned and played—and the one that really got me started collecting dulcimers—was made by Wade Martin, the master carver from Swannanoa, North Carolina. I bought my Wade Martin dulcimer in the summer of 1952. Wade was then a professional baseball player in Rocky Mount, North Carolina, but did carving in the off-season. His delightful small carvings of animals and people were an attraction at the Allanstand Craft Shop in Asheville.

Wade came from a family of renowned fiddlers and fiddle makers, including his father, Marcus Martin, a fine traditional fiddler.

I made friends with Marcus when we both performed in 1952 at Bascom Lunsford's annual Mountain Dance and Folk Festival in Asheville. At the time, I was still playing the autoharp.

Marcus mentioned to me an instrument that someone had brought to the Martins after finding it in an old barn. This turned out to be a dulcimer, but at first none of the Martins knew anything about it. They didn't know what it was or who had made it or what. They also had never heard such an instrument played. Wade, however, made a copy of this "found" dulcimer, and he began to sell his dulcimers in Asheville.

I took my Wade Martin dulcimer home, "fiddled with it," and tried to learn what I could about dulcimer history. I had seen photographs of people playing dulcimers in books like Jean Thomas's *The Singin' Gatherin', Tunes from the Southern Appalachians.* Also the Ritchie family and John Jacob Niles used dulcimers. But I really didn't know much about the dulcimer, and it seemed nobody else did either. Dulcimers were not from the British Isles, although most of the songs traditional in Ohio and the Midwest are of British origin. And, at least in the folk music field, nobody associated dulcimers with Ohio. However, I was to discover a dulcimer tradition in Ohio as old and as real as that found in the states of the southern Appalachians.

I wrote to Wade telling him of my growing interest in dulcimers and asking if he would make me some new tuning pegs for his dulcimer, which was made of sumac, a very beautiful wood. Along with the pegs came a letter from him saying:

> These screws are made of a real hard wood, locust. It is as near the color of sumac as I could get, and I believe they will hold up good. You may have to sand them down a little to fit. They will hold better if you put some black board school chalk on them when you put them in the Dulcimer. I'm sure they will be alright. . . . I have two orders for Dulcimers, and the sumac wood is so scarce. I don't know if I can fill them or not. There's only one place we know, and there's very little left. I'm afraid we won't be able to make but very few more sumac Dulcimers.

Then Marcus wrote me early in 1953 to say that he had just finished making a dulcimer of sumac, cypress, and basswood, also modeled on the original "found" dulcimer. He asked if I would be interested in it, and of course I was. My Martin Marcus dulcimer is almost the same shape as the one Wade made.

Beautifully carved and carefully made, the Wade and Marcus Martin dulcimers are among the best of their era.

Jane Jones McNerlin holding the dulcimer made by her husband, John, in Oak Hill, Ohio, 1953. Photo by James W. Grimes

28 Jane Jones McNerlin and the McNerlin Family Dulcimers

When the Roll Is Called Up Yonder

JACKSON COUNTY

JANE JONES McNerlin, of Oak Hill in Jackson County, Ohio, surprised me by holding her dulcimer pegs-down against her shoulder in an inclined position. So far as I knew, the instrument was played that way nowhere else. To Mrs. McNerlin, however, this was the only way: the way her father and her grandfather held and played the dulcimer, and the way Mrs. McNerlin herself taught her daughter, Roma, to play.

Jane's dulcimer was made by her husband, John McNerlin, who patterned it on the dulcimer that had been owned by her grandfather. Jimmie made a detailed pencil drawing with measurements of the John McNerlin dulcimer. He also later did an oil painting portrait of John McNerlin, which he gave to the McNerlin family.

When we visited Jane, the dulcimer that her grandfather, Richard Jones, played was in the home of Jane's sister, who also lived in Oak Hill. Family lore had it that her grandfather might have brought his dulcimer with him from his native Wales, where he had been a music teacher. But probably he picked it up along the way to Jackson County after he arrived in America around 1850.

I did wonder if Jane's unusual way of playing that she learned from her grandfather might have been an outgrowth from the playing of the ancient obsolete bowed Welsh instrument, the crwth. The McNerlins had seen others in the area play with the dulcimer on a table or ironing board, but she carried on her own family's traditional style of playing. For some of my performance pieces, like "Hush, My Babe," I adopted the McNerlin family style of holding the dulcimer, but I never met or heard of another dulcimer player who played it that way.

After the deaths of Jane and John McNerlin and their daughter, Roma, both dulcimers were inherited by Roma's son, Daryl, with whom I had some correspondence. In a house fire in 1989, Daryl told me, he lost almost everything he owned—including Jimmie's portrait of John McNerlin. However, the original heirloom dulcimer survived, and Daryl donated it in 1995 to the Ohio Historical Society. The dulcimer is on display at the Campus Martius Museum in Marietta, Ohio.

The author leads the singing of "The Star-Spangled Banner" at the National Folk Festival at St. Louis, Missouri, in 1952. Photo by Eugene Taylor reproduced by permission from Ralph E. Taylor. Anne Grimes Collection, American Folklife Center, Library of Congress

29 The National Folk Festival at St. Louis

May Kennedy McCord, Jenny Wells Vincent, Pete Seeger

Hangman • I Am a Soldier of Pancho Villa • Jefferson and Liberty

WHEN I PERFORMED at the National Folk Festival in 1952, I played my autoharp and sang folksongs from Ohio, including the abolitionist song "Ohio River Blues." I was also honored to lead the singing of "The Star-Spangled Banner" at the festival's closing ceremonies, introduced by Sarah Gertrude Knott, founder of the National Folk Festival.

We did lots of sharing and singing at the festival, so the next year, when the festival again was held at Kiel Auditorium in St. Louis, I hauled along my tape recorder—that great big thing—to collect a number of treasures. They included backstage singing by many fine performers including Pete Seeger, May Kennedy McCord, Fred High, Booth Campbell, and Jenny Wells Vincent.

May Kennedy McCord, the "Queen of the Ozarks," was a marvelous lady and a friend and role model. She was someone who knew everybody, and of course she loved people, and they loved her. She recorded more than one hundred ballads for the Library of Congress and contributed some seventy items to Vance Randolph's four-volume *Ozark Folksongs*. She also contributed to Carl Sandburg's *New American Songbag*.

Knowing that May McCord and Carl Sandburg were good friends, and that I would soon be seeing him in Columbus, I suggested to May that she might like to send a taped greeting. One week later, Carl Sandburg was in my home, listening to a tape recording of May McCord singing for him "Hangman," "Lass of Roch Royal," and "Chilly Winds."

Tape-recording May's greeting for Carl Sandburg was a high point of the 1953 festival for me. We were in a bare dressing room, the acoustics were not the best, and I was new to tape-recording. But through it all came the heartfelt warmth of May's greetings—the authenticity of her singing and the inspiration of her friendship.

Booth Campbell and Fred High were rare characters, both in their eighties. Being squired around St. Louis by these fine gentlemen from the Ozarks was an experience I will always remember. From Cane Hill, Arkansas, Booth sang "Lorena," a favorite of Confederate soldiers and a lovely song.

A wonderful traditional singer from Berryville, Arkansas, Fred High came from a family that had lived in Ohio for a couple of generations before they moved south. Fred was also an author and collector of songs, published in his *Old, Old Folk Songs.* His third book, *It Happened in the Ozarks,* published in 1954, includes a photograph of me playing the dulcimer, an instrument Fred said he did not see growing up in the Ozarks. Among the songs I taped Fred singing was a complete version of the Child ballad "The House Carpenter."

May Kennedy McCord on the cover of the December 7, 1954, Bias, Springfield's Weekly Newsjournal. *Photo by Vera Thompson. Inscription to the author reproduced with permission from Henry Janss*

Jenny Wells Vincent, of New Mexico, who specializes in music of the American Southwest, sang "I Am a Soldier of Pancho Villa," a song that celebrates the Mexican folk hero. Vincent's spirited "Pancho Villa" later could be heard sung around our household, since our kids loved it.

Pete Seeger was just like a pied piper—he could get thousands of people to sing. Among the songs Pete sang at our hootenanny party backstage were "Jefferson and Liberty," "Pick a Bale of Cotton," "Hunters of Kentucky," and "Ida Red." Accompanying our singing on his signature banjo, Pete also led the group in "Hey Li Lee Lo" with verses I had written down about my five kids, which was fun.

"Wyoming Jack" O'Brien (left) and Harry Belafonte with the author, who holds the Wade Martin dulcimer, St. Louis, Missouri, 1953. Reproduced by permission from the St. Louis Globe-Democrat Archives of the St. Louis Mercantile Library at the University of Missouri–St. Louis

Hangman (The Maid Freed from the Gallows; Child #95)

"Hangman, hangman, slack your rope,
Slacken it for a while.
I think I see my father coming;
He's traveled for many a mile.

"Oh father, have you brought me money?
And have you come to pay my fee?
Or have you come to see me hanging
High on the gallows tree?"

"No son, I've brought you none nor gold,
And I have not come to pay your fee.
But I have come to see you hanging
High on the gallows tree."

"Hangman, hangman, slack your rope,
Slacken it for a while.
I think I see my mother coming;
She's traveled for many a mile.

"Oh mother, have you brought me gold?
And have you come to pay my fee?
Or have you come to see me hanging
High on the gallows tree?"

"Oh no, my son, I have no gold,
 And I've not come to pay your fee.
 But I must stand and see you hanging
 High on the gallows tree."

"Hangman, hangman, slack your rope,
 Slacken it for a while.
 I think I see my true-love coming;
 Travelin' for many a mile.

"Oh true-love, have you brought me gold?
 And have you come to pay my fee?
 Or have you come to see me hanging
 High on the gallows tree?"

"Oh yes, my love, I've brought you money,
 And I have come to pay your fee.
 And I will never see you hanging
 High on the gallows tree."

I Am a Soldier of Pancho Villa

I am a soldier of Pancho Villa
Of his dorados I am but one.
It matters not if my life is taken
I'll fight for him 'til the battle's done.

He is here, he has come
Pancho Villa con su gente,
Con sus dorados valiente
Que por él han de morir.

Ya aquella gran División del Norte
Solo unos cuantos quedamos ya,
Subiendo tierras, bajando montes
Salo buscando con quién pelear.

Ya llegó, ya está aquí
Pancho Villa con su gente,
Con sus dorados valientes
Que por él han de morir.

Ya centinela pasó revista
El campamento ya se durmió.
Adios, les dice este Villista,
Ya nos veremos otra ocasión.

He has come, he is here
Pancho Villa with his people,
With his followers valiant
Who for him gladly would die.

Jefferson and Liberty

The gloomy night before us flies;
Its reign of terror now is o'er.
Its gags, inquisitors, and spies,
Its herds of harpies are no more.

Rejoice, Columbia's sons, rejoice!
To tyrants never bend the knee,
But join with heart and soul and voice
For Jefferson and Liberty.

No lordling here with gorging jaws
Shall wring from industry the food;
Nor fiery bigot's holy laws
Lay waste our fields and streets with blood.

Rejoice, Columbia's sons, rejoice!
To tyrants never bend the knee,
But join with heart and soul and voice
For Jefferson and Liberty.

Here strangers from a thousand shores
Compelled by tyranny to roam
Shall find amidst abundant stores
A nobler and a happier home.

Rejoice, Columbia's sons, rejoice!
To tyrants never bend the knee,
But join with heart and soul and voice
For Jefferson and Liberty.

Rejoice, Columbia's sons, rejoice!
To tyrants never bend the knee,
But join with heart and soul and voice
For Jefferson and Liberty.

Neva Randolph at the Thompson, Warrick, Workman Family Reunion in Murray City, Ohio, 1941 or 1942. Photo courtesy of Forest J. Farmer, Sr.

30 Neva Randolph

My Station's Gonna Be Changed • *Shine on Me*

HOCKING COUNTY

THE GRANDDAUGHTER of freed slaves who had settled in Logan, Ohio, Neva Randolph was born in Logan in 1874. Her reputation as a fine singer had been known to me for some time when I finally managed, in 1953, to make the drive down to Murray City in Hocking County to see her—only to learn that she was on her deathbed! A lot of cars were parked in front of the house, and her daughter told us that the people had come to pay their last respects to a beloved and well-respected friend.

I asked—since we had come such a long way—if I might just sing to Mrs. Randolph. Her daughter agreed, and we were escorted into a room where Mrs. Randolph lay in bed, surrounded by friends and family. I sang a few ballads, like "Barbara Allen."

Mrs. Randolph responded. She said she knew the ballads I sang, but her parents had never let her sing or even learn such "worldly songs," as she called them. She added that she was glad to hear them again—and then she began singing herself!

Her daughter and the neighbors were astounded, and we got out the tape recorder.

Mrs. Randolph's singing especially interested me, since her style resembled the "old style" or "lining out" hymn-singing practiced by both black and white church congregations, reflections of which I found in traditional singing. Her "My Station's Gonna Be Changed" she associated with the Underground Railroad—the popular name for the system that helped fugitive slaves reach freedom in Canada. Another of her songs, "Shine on Me," is a traditional spiritual.

On the day we visited her, even under the circumstances, Neva Randolph's unusually beautiful voice had a strength, warmth, and quality equal to that of a concert singer.

During our visit, Mrs. Randolph practically came back to life—very dramatically. Before we left, although she had been down flat in bed when we went there, she was sitting up in bed singing, and asking us to come back again.

My Station's Gonna Be Changed

Oh, the station's gonna be changed after 'while.
Oh, the station's gonna be changed after 'while.
When the Lord Himself shall come
And shall say, "Your work is done."
Oh, your station will be changed after 'while.

The Gospel train is coming.
It's coming around the curve.
Stopping at every station,
Straining every nerve.
Get your ticket ready.
Prepare to get on board.
For your station's gonna be changed after 'while.

Oh, your station's gonna be changed after 'while.
Oh, my station's gonna be changed after 'while.
When the Lord Himself shall come,
And shall say, "Your work is done."
Oh, your station will be changed after 'while.

Shine on Me

Chorus:
Shine on me; shine on me.
I wonder if the lighthouse will shine on me.
Shine on me; shine on me.
I wonder if the lighthouse will shine on me.

I heard the voice of Jesus saying,
"Come on to me and rest.
Lie down thy weary one, lie down
Thine head upon my breast."
Chorus

Give me the grace to run this race,
Increase my courage, Lord.
I want 'a make Heaven my hiding place
That'll lead me on to God.
Chorus

Arbannah and Eli "Babe" Reno. Photo courtesy of Ottie W. Reno

31 Eli "Babe" Reno

Rarden Wreck · Portsmouth Fellows

SCIOTO
COUNTY

I FOUND ELI "BABE" Reno and his wife, Arbannah, in 1953 living in the country in Scioto County. Their home was on top of a hill in an apple orchard in the same place his grandfather settled after coming from Scotland. It was beautiful.

They lived almost as in pioneer times, and, since they had no electricity, we recorded in the home of their son, Ottie, who was a lawyer practicing in nearby Waverly. Babe sang and played the banjo, and "Banna" stood behind him singing like a steam calliope. They were a wonderful couple, fun and intelligent.

Babe Reno was well known in Pike and Scioto counties as a singer of old-time songs. In his late sixties when I recorded him, Reno claimed to know more than three hundred songs, many of which he had written down. He learned some from his parents and some from people in the community.

Babe's "Rarden Wreck" tells of a terrible railroad wreck in 1893 on the C. P. *&* V. (Cincinnati, Portsmouth and Virginia Railroad) at the town of Rarden, Ohio, a few miles from where the Renos lived. Both the ballad and the train wreck in Rarden were widely remembered in southern Ohio at the time I recorded the Renos.

The ballad is fashioned after and to the tune of "The Ship That Never Returned" by the nineteenth-century American songwriter Henry Clay Work.

Another wonderful song Babe sang was "The Cigarette Song," which he had learned years before from Parson Peyton Crabtree at a "dry meeting" in Portsmouth, Ohio. I later learned it had been sung in Primitive churches and at Salvation Army gatherings in the area. This is the song Carl Sandburg so enjoyed when I sang it for him at his eightieth birthday party.

Babe Reno's fine "Portsmouth Fellows" is an Ohio version of a widely traditional old English nursery song known variously by such titles as "Beau Reynard," "Bold Rangers," or "The Jolly Huntsmen."

I got on to Babe Reno through Vic Newton, a popular folk radio personality I went to see in Piketon, Ohio, in Scioto County. It turned out Newton sang sentimental religious and hillbilly songs that didn't interest me. So I sang him some songs, and he said, "What you have to do is go see Babe Reno; he sings your kind of songs."

Rarden Wreck

One Sunday's morn when the wind was sighing
Through the branches of the trees,
A train pulled out from Cincinnati
On the old C. P. and V.

They were switching cars, and they gave the back-up signal,
And the engine it took slack.
They knew it not was the last trip eastward
For the train that never come back.

Did she ever return? No, she never returned,
And that's why she never returned.
For they ran through a switch at Rarden Station,
And that's why she never returned.

"Just one more trip," said Fireman Little,
As he boarded forty-five,
"Then I'll go back to Cincinnati."
But he never got back alive.

He was shoveling coal in the fiery furnace,
And his face it was all black.
But he got killed at Rarden Station,
And that's why he never come back.

The engineer was poor George Glascoe.
He was pulling forty-four.
Little did he think when he left Portsmouth
He would pull that train no more.

He was running into Rarden Station
Eleven minutes late,
When Glascoe saw that the switch was open—
Leaped blindly to his fate.

Did he ever return? No, he never returned,
And that's why he never returned.
For he got killed at Rarden Station,
And that's why he never returned.

Portsmouth Fellows

Come, all you Portsmouth fellows,
Let's go and hunt a fox.
Let's go and hunt bold ranger
Among the hills and rocks.

Chorus:
Come a whoop, whoop a whoop an' a high-lo.
We will join the merry strands.
Come a' ran, tan, tan,
Come a' rip, a tip, a tan.
Come away, oh, rise-oh, dogs we run.
And through the woods we go, gay boys,
And through the woods we run!

The next I saw was an old man
A'plowing up his ground.
He said he saw bold ranger
As he played 'round and 'round.
Chorus

The next I saw was an old lady
A'combing up her locks.
She said she saw bold ranger
Among the hills and rocks.
Chorus

32 Branch Rickey

"Luck Is the Residue of Design"

SCIOTO COUNTY

BRANCH RICKEY'S LONG career as a baseball executive included developing dynasties for the Brooklyn Dodgers, the St. Louis Cardinals, and the Pittsburgh Pirates. His hiring of Jackie Robinson for the Dodgers broke the color barrier in major league baseball in 1947.

I tape-recorded Rickey in 1954 at the home of his daughter, Mary Eckler, a friend and neighbor of ours in Upper Arlington. There he contributed a song from his native Scioto County, Ohio, where he grew up in the late nineteenth century on a farm along Duck Run near Lucasville. It was just a short fragment he said he heard as a boy sung at revival meetings in an African American settlement "back in the hills out of Davis Station."

In a story about Branch Rickey published in 1958 by the Ohio Valley Folklore Press, Rickey shared much more about his life growing up on a family farm in southern Ohio. As a teenager, Rickey said, he had grown tired of the "humdrum" of school. So he asked his father if he might quit school and go to work. His father assented, sending him to plant corn five miles into the hills on Duck Creek for four days—a tough experience that changed Branch Rickey's mind about school. But it also left him with the dilemma of how to save face with his family and take back everything he had said just a week before about not wanting to go to school.

"Father made it very easy for me," Rickey said.

> He repeated all his arguments with greater strength and force and put the matter up in such form that I would simply have to give up to parental authority. That was a great "out" for me. Thus I, with apparent regret and, of course, with a show of contrite hesitation, consented to do as he said and go back to school. This is what Dad had planned all the time. He was a wonderful father.

After graduating from Ohio Wesleyan University, Rickey earned a law degree from the University of Michigan (where he also served from 1910 to 1913 as baseball coach) before embarking on his professional baseball career. He also was in demand as an inspirational speaker for stories like his "Luck Is the Residue of Design."

"That's a good story, it's a corking story," Rickey said as—prodded on by Mary Eckler—he shared the story with us in the Eckler home in Upper Arlington.

"Luck Is the Residue of Design"

The story Branch Rickey told to family and friends in Upper Arlington, Ohio, in 1954 centers around a game played some twenty-eight years earlier between Michigan and Minnesota for the Little Brown Jug, one of the oldest rivalries in football. The win also assured Michigan a share of the Big Ten Championship. Set in winter 1926–27, the story takes its moral from the way underdog Michigan prepared for the game. The story picks up here with Rickey happening to run into Harry Kipke, the Michigan assistant coach under Coach Fielding Yost, in an old inn in Michigan.

. . . One of the most spectacular games that has ever been played.

Well, I met Harry Kipke. I was up in north Michigan, and he was up there making some speeches and I was up there hunting, up in the peninsula. And I strolled into a little old country inn, village hotel, one night, about dark, and there sat Kipke over there in a big leather chair. Well, [I said] "It was a great." . . . It was only a couple of weeks before [after] this game, you know. I congratulated him. And there was a little old wizened-up fellow about 75 years old with a beard and scraggly and wasn't weighing not more than 130 pounds, and he was sitting in the next chair.

And I sat down here and we were just going to town about the game and winning the championship, and how they beat Minnesota—and how they ran the 95 yards and beat them 7–6 in the Little Brown Jug, you know, down in Ann Arbor. And we were just having a pretty good time. And this little old bird over there jumped up:

"I can't stand it any longer." He said: "You men talking about that game." Says, "You know all about it . . ."

Then he went right through the statistics, and he ridiculed us and he said: "There was no time in the game that Michigan had a chance to win." He said, "You gloat over it and brag about it." He said, "You were beaten from start to finish. It was a fluke."

And then he went ahead and he told how this fellow [Bennie] Oosterbaan had violated all the elemental principles of coaching, and that he had failed to fall on the ball as he should have done.

"Fumbled footballs, you are supposed to fall on them," said the little old fella.

So at that point he got up, and very angry he was, he stalked out of the lobby.

And Harry turned to me, and he said, "You know, the old fellow's right. The statistics are all just as he says." He said,

"Everything was in their favor. We never had the ball on their end of the field during the ball game. We only made one or two first downs."

He said, "Everything was against us. But," he said, "he doesn't know all the story."

He said, "The week before we played Minnesota, the old coach, Frank Yost, called us all together and he said, 'Boys, the way that the games have been going lately,' he said, 'we don't have a chance to beat Minnesota.' He said, 'I think you've got to play on the breaks. I think you've got to play on the chances of the game.'"

And he says that as a result of that, the coaching staff had meetings and he said on Monday morning we started out and he said we put Oosterbaan and [William] Flora, the two All-American ends, running up and down the field all week long, never in any scrimmage, with the managers and assistant managers and substitutes with their arms full of footballs throwing them to these fellows running. "And they were never to fall on them. They were to scoop them up and keep running." He said it got so that Oosterbaan with those tremendous big hands of his could take one in one hand and one in another on a dead run and just keep right on going, picking up rolling footballs on the Ann Arbor football field. And he said he was remarkable. And so was Flora. But, he said, he was instructed not to fall on any football, and so was every other man on the team.

"Take a chance getting away with a fumble. We need to do it. We've got to have these breaks in our favor to win this game."

He said, "The old gentleman just doesn't know that that was according to plan. And while he said it was all luck and all the break of chance and that all the good fortune was on the side of Michigan," he said, "that thing was the result of perfect planning."

It was true, he says, that Oosterbaan's great agility and speed enabled him to get away and run the 95 yards. But he said he was never under the fundamental instruction of falling on a rolling, a free football.

And I use the story as saying that sometimes you've got to do all you can and what's left over is good luck. If you've done every living human thing you can to make a thing come out a certain way, well, what's left over is ordinarily good luck. And when you're negligent or careless or you don't do all the things or you don't go according to plan, well, the thing that happens sometimes isn't in your favor so much, it's bad luck.

And here was a thing that was right according to program—in which every man did every living human thing he
could do. And what happened was what was left over of the
plan. And I called it some years ago in a talk I made in giving
that thing as an illustration—I called it what Mary has just
referred to here—as the "Residue of Design."

That's what luck is and you want to keep it there. You don't
want to abandon your plan. You go ahead with it. And you
work for it—do everything you can do to bring it around.
Well, there are a lot of incidentals that you can't anticipate or
understand, or maybe control at all, that happen as a result of
your pursuing a plan. Well, it can be good luck or it can be bad
luck, and it depends on what. But in any event, you've got to
put it over to where it belongs, you see. It's what's left over.
It's not the determining thing. It isn't a part of the elemental
purpose at all. It's really incidental to what you are doing, and
I call it the residue of design. You see?

Carl Sandburg with the author at his Connemara Farm, Flat Rock, North Carolina, 1956. Photo by Steve Grimes

33 Carl Sandburg

Record Makers

THE POET CARL SANDBURG was always interested in songs. My mother, who was a huge fan of his poetry, owned a 1927 first edition of Sandburg's *The American Songbag,* one of the earliest published collections of American folk music. He dedicated it "to those unknown singers—who made songs—out of love, fun, grief—and to those many other singers—who kept those songs as living things of the heart and mind—out of love, fun, grief."

In 1952 after performing in the Mountain Dance and Folk Festival in Asheville, North Carolina, I showed up unannounced at Sandburg's door at his Connemara Farm south of Asheville. I had with me a letter of introduction from my friend and mentor, Mary O. Eddy, the Perrysville, Ohio, folklorist who was among those Sandburg consulted in his research for *The American Songbag.* His wife came to the door and took the letter. In a few minutes, Sandburg came bounding down to welcome me in.

The next year, when Sandburg came to Ohio to lecture at Ohio Wesleyan and Ohio State University, he was guest of honor at a party Jimmie and I hosted at our home in Upper Arlington. There I tape-recorded him singing songs and sharing stories, including ones related to his research on his Pulitzer Prize–winning series of biographies of Abraham Lincoln.

A highlight of the evening was Sandburg's listening and responding to greetings from May Kennedy McCord that I had tape-recorded a week earlier at the 1953 National Folk Festival in St. Louis.

"This is May Kennedy McCord," we heard her say, "and I'm doing this mostest for Carl Sandburg. I think maybe he'd like this old version of mine in the hills. Bless his heart, I wish I could see him." We listened as she sang "Hangman," "Lass of Roch Royal," and "Chilly Winds."

Sandburg responded with a tape recording of his own:

"You're blessing my heart, and now I'm blessing your heart," he said to introduce several songs he sang for May McCord. He started with "Record Makers," which he said had been sung by a Salvation Army lass on the street corner of his hometown of Galesburg, Illinois. Sandburg also sang, "I'm Sad and I'm Lonely," which was included in the 1927 edition of *The American Songbag*.

I later managed to splice the two taped greetings together and send them off to Sandburg and McCord. These two friends had much in common. As pioneer collectors of our nation's musical heritage, they not only wrote about it and published it, but as they became distinguished they continued to sing. They retained their eagerness to listen and to learn, as well as to savor the joys of sharing their wisdom—wisdom seasoned with simplicity and humor and projected with outstanding charm.

At my party, Sandburg also was gracious enough to sign my mother's copy of his book, which remains a family treasure.

Several years later, I returned to Connemara Farm. Sandburg and I sang and played our dulcimers. He asked if I had ever considered doing recordings, and that he thought my material, along with my dulcimer discoveries, should be more widely known. His remarks helped me screw up my courage to take the plunge to make my album for Folkways.

The last time I saw Carl Sandburg was at his eightieth birthday party in 1958 at the home of our mutual friend Mary Zimmerman in Bexley, Ohio. I sang for him "The Cigarette Song," which I had collected from Eli "Babe" Reno. I remember Sandburg's saying, "Oh, Lincoln would have loved that."

Record Makers

As we roll along we all are record makers,
Records black and white, in the wrong or right.
As we roll along we all are record makers.
Oh, be ready when the train comes in.

Records black and white, in the wrong or right.
As we roll along we all are record makers.
Oh, be ready when the train comes in.

Arthur D. Tyler with his dulcimer in Columbus, Ohio, 1954.
Photo by James W. Grimes

34 Arthur D. Tyler and the Tyler Dulcimer

Darling Nelly Gray

FRANKLIN
COUNTY

MY FIRST DULCIMER exhibit was in 1955 at the Ohio Historical Museum in Columbus. Of all the instruments there, the one made by Arthur Tyler of Galloway in central Ohio's Franklin County was outstanding, both for its fine workmanship and for its importance in musical Americana.

Typical of one type of Ohio dulcimer in that it looked like a long, skinny fiddle, Tyler's dulcimer was made of white pine and hickory poplar with a tailpiece of cedar. It was remarkable for its nicety of detail and the sensitive relationships of its parts, its top scroll beautifully carved.

Tyler made his first dulcimer in 1894 in Galloway when he was just seventeen, and he liked it so much he made four more that same year. Like all other makers and players, Tyler had to have a model, since the dulcimer was not made in factories and was very rarely sold out of the family of the maker. He modeled the ones he made on one that a cousin in nearby Grove City got from an itinerant farm worker who was originally from McArthur in Vinton County.

Later, I was to discover in Vinton and surrounding southeastern Ohio counties a nest of dulcimer players, some with dulcimers very similar in design to Tyler's. In that area, the dulcimer was often referred to as "dulcerine," and that is how Tyler also referred to the instrument.

Tyler told me that the word "dulcerine" distinguished the instrument from another instrument popular at that time, the factory-made "hammered dulcimer"—the instrument with a number of strings, like a zither, that is played with little hammers.

I found Tyler and his "dulcerine" in the early 1950s when I gave a lecture-recital in Chillicothe, Ohio. A woman in the audience remembered that as a young schoolteacher in the 1930s in Galloway she had heard the father of one of her students play an instrument similar to the one I played. She remembered the family name, and told me about Tyler.

To discover a dulcimer player who had played in relative isolation an instrument that he had made some sixty years before—and only few minutes' drive from my home—was a high point in my dulcimer search.

For his part, Tyler was astounded to know that anyone else had a dulcimer. He had seen another one only once. That was in 1919 at a Methodist Centenary celebration at the Ohio State Fairgrounds in Columbus where he saw a dulcimer in a mountain school display, but could find no one who knew what it was or how to play it. He was even more excited when he came to my house and saw my dulcimer collection, then numbering fifteen.

For many years after our meeting, Tyler was a feature of Ohio Folklore Society gatherings. He put his dulcimer on a table and stood up to play it. This is often done, although an instrument so played usually has little wooden "feet" on the bottom that Tyler's did not have. He used a round stick to fret, and plucked with a piece of whalebone from an old corset stay or a whittled piece of wood. Hymns and old favorites like "Home Sweet Home" and "Turkey in the Straw" were his selections, played in a straightforward melodic style.

Tyler also played an instrumental version of the internationally known and loved abolitionist song, "Darling Nelly Gray."

Sunday MAGAZINE AUGUST 4, 1957

SONGS OUT OF THE PAST
Preserving Ohio's Folklore (SEE PAGE 8)

Columbus Dispatch Sunday Magazine *cover photo of Arthur D. Tyler,
August 4, 1957. Photo by Mac Shaffer courtesy of the* Columbus Dispatch

Composed in 1856 by Ohioan Benjamin Russell Hanby, the lyrics
were inspired by the story of an escaped slave who died in 1842
in Rushville, Ohio. The song lived long after its association with
the pre–Civil War period. As it became traditional, its text became
slightly changed and, in fact, came to be most often heard in a
square dance call.

Over the years, Tyler lost track of two of his five dulcimers
through lending them around the community. He still had two, and
I purchased the third from Warren Reed, of Grove City, Ohio, for
whom Tyler had made it in 1894.

35 William T. Utter and Scheitholts from Licking County

LICKING COUNTY

DR. WILLIAM T. UTTER, professor and chair of history at Denison University in Granville, Licking County, Ohio, joined in the start of my collection of dulcimers and traditional plucked instruments when in 1952 he gave me a scheitholt that he had found in Licking County.

A scheitholt is the long, narrow, straight-sided zither with frets that some scholars link to the mysterious origin of the American dulcimer. Originating in Germany, scheitholts were not uncommon in the Pennsylvania "Dutch" areas, and from the early 1800s they also were traditionally played in the Welsh Hills of Licking County in Ohio.

A fine musician (on bassoon and flute), a collector of antique flutes, and a cabinetmaker, Bill restored his scheitholt before he gave it to me. He had purchased it from a Granville man who had it in his attic for thirty years after getting it "a long time ago" in Johnstown in Licking County. It is a particularly nice instrument, with fine cabinetwork and exquisite sound holes.

In 1965 I added to my collection another scheitholt that I got from Robbins Hunter, an antique dealer in Granville. Robbins told me he had purchased it at a sale at the Granville house of Myrtle Tilton, who was born in 1876 and died in 1961. The story is that Myrtle's father, Sidney A. Tilton, an herbalist born in Ohio in 1844, made the instrument for her when she was a girl, and that Myrtle and her father sometimes gave concerts—she on the scheitholt and he on the fiddle.

Bill Utter was one of several recognized scholars in Ohio academe who encouraged what I was doing in developing a collection of Ohio folk music. Moreover, he and his wife, Alma, were our long-time friends. I had known Bill and Alma since the 1920s, when he was getting his doctorate and teaching at Ohio State University in Columbus. The Utters lived near my parents, and both our families were active in nearby Indianola Methodist Church.

Later, Jimmie and Bill became friends through their work in the Ohio Historical Society. Our friendship and admiration for the Utters influenced our decision to move from Upper Arlington to Granville in 1962 after Jimmie became chair of the Fine Arts Department at Denison University.

Another instrument Bill Utter contributed to my collection is a little gem—a fretless box zither which he called an Aeolian or "wind" harp. He told me it had been owned by a Licking County family who put it in lowered windows to make "ghostly" music when the wind blew.

(top left) Scheitholt found in Johnstown, Licking County, Ohio. Photo by Robert Force reproduced with permission

(middle left) Scheitholt made by Sidney A. Tilton in Licking County, Ohio. Photo by Robert Force reproduced with permission

(bottom left) Aeolian wind harp found in Licking County, Ohio. Photographer unknown

Bessie Weinrich with the author in Vigo, Ohio, ca. 1953.
Photos by James W. Grimes. Anne Grimes Collection,
American Folklife Center, Library of Congress

36 Bessie Weinrich

The Miller's Will • The Fox • States and Capitals •
Crockery Ware • My Eyes Are Dim • The Big Shirt

ROSS
COUNTY

BESSIE WEINRICH—gosh, she was wonderful. She taped forty-seven items for my collection, all important. A fine singer in the old style whose family songs included rare English ballads, Bessie was not only a major contributor but a dear friend. She loved helping me memorize and sing her songs, and arrange dulcimer accompaniment. The photographs of Bessie and me singing lustily together are some of my favorites.

Bessie lived with her husband, Phil, in the tiny village of Vigo in Ross County, Ohio, not far from where Salt Creek flows into the

Bessie and Philip Weinrich in Vigo, Ohio, ca. 1953.
Photo by James W. Grimes

Scioto River. Vigo had a few "downtown" buildings with houses clustered on surrounding steep hills. Bessie and Phil lived in a large and comfortable home frequently visited by family and neighbors. It was full of gorgeous antiques as well as many items she had made, including woven carpets—even stair carpets. They had a fine garden and many pet cats.

Bessie was always interested in what I could learn about the songs she sang and in hearing about previously known versions of "her" songs, such as "The Miller's Will," a story about a miller's deciding to which of three sons to leave his gristmill.

Born in Ross County in 1881, Bessie was descended from English Cavaliers who settled in Virginia before moving to Ohio. They were a family of millers. Her father, Paul H. Jones, was a miller, and her mother, Luella Dixon Jones, came from a Ross County settler family that had operated mills for generations.

Bessie even met her husband through the mill: "Now Phil, that's how I fell in love with him. He was going to the mill with a sack of corn on his back and he was the cutest darn thing."

"The Miller's Will" was a seventeenth-century English broadside also known as "The Dishonest Miller" or "The Miller's Advice to His Three Sons." One of the most interesting things about Bessie's version of this song was the refrain. The more typically collected refrain includes nonsense syllables, such as "foll-loll-de-ay," or "phi, tra-la-diddle, dumpy dee." That Bessie came from a family of millers may account for the logical, and possibly original, refrain in her version, "Rye, fodder, and hay."

When I performed at the New Century Club in Chillicothe in 1954, I was singing on stage in my pioneer costume, and Bessie was in the audience. I invited her to join me in singing her version of "The Miller's Will." The song has some "cuss words," and afterward

Bessie proudly said to me: "You could sing it without those words. But that's the way they sang it!"

Another classic Bessie sang was "The Fox," also known as "The Black Duck" and "The Fox and the Goose." The strong midwestern tradition of this British nursery song was helped by songsters, sheet music, and tavern entertainers, and I collected it throughout the state.

She also sang a little song she learned in school, "States and Capitals," which features—and teaches—the major rivers on which state capitals are located. Bessie recalled that in school when they were feeling "kind of smothered," their teacher took them outside to learn their "geographies and histories" while sitting atop an old barn.

Bessie learned most of her songs from her mother, Luella Dixon Jones, who was born in 1862 in Ross County on Salt Creek.

"I was all the kids she had, and I was very much spoiled.... She'd just sing them to me, teach me everything she knew," Bessie told me.

Her mother kept what Bessie called a "ballot book" of songs from her family and others in the community. Bessie sometimes referred to her mother's book, as when she sang "Crockery Ware." After singing the song, she read her mother's notation about it: "This I heard my father's mother's sister sing in 1886. She was Betsy Boblett."

Both Bessie and another important contributor, Bessie's cousin Ellie Flack, remembered Betsy Boblett (who was Bessie's great-great-aunt and Ellie's grandmother) singing "Crockery Ware" and other songs at family feasts. Various folk scholars have identified "Crockery Ware," the rare bawdy ballad about a chamber-pot trap to catch an unwelcome lover, as possibly a late seventeenth-century broadside ballad.

Bessie also learned songs from her father. A favorite of his was "My Eyes Are Dim," a parody on the lining-out of hymns in church practiced in the early congregational oral tradition. The verses of the song alternate between speaking and the singing. Bessie's delivery started:

"So the preacher got up and he would always read the song and then the congregation would sing. And he got up and he got his Bible out and he said, 'My eyes are dim, I cannot see, I left my specs at home.'" Then Bessie completed the verse by singing the words as if she were the congregation responding to the preacher's lead: "My eyes are dim, I cannot see, I left my specs at home."

The song, in spoken and sung verses, goes on from there. Many people in Ohio have different versions of this story, and some claim that it actually happened.

In Bessie's family nearly everyone sang or played an instrument, or both. Bessie played the fiddle. "I didn't take lessons. Anything I'd ever hear, I would get the fiddle and play it." Bessie also danced. "I was just a kid, but everybody danced with me . . . square dancing and schottische. Nobody can schottische anymore. . . . I wish to the Lord I could teach somebody that old schottische."

The family also enjoyed going to shows that came to "The Brick," the main downtown building in Vigo, as well as tent shows that featured medicine shows and other forms of entertainment and religion. At one of the tent shows, they heard a man sing "Si Hubbard" ("Hey Rube"), a song that so interested her father that he asked the performer to write down the words for him. I taped Bessie singing her "Hey Rube," a very long song about two farmer boys at a fair that get snookered—I mean they really got cheated, had a terrible time.

I thought "Hey Rube" was a bunch of "corn"—because she had all these marvelous English ballads. But later, I invited my colleague and friend Claude Simpson, who was teaching English at Ohio State at that time, to come over and listen to my Bessie Weinrich tape. When we got to "Hey Rube," I said I thought we'd better just erase that. Claude said, "Wait up! Wait up! It took Carl Sandburg three people to get the whole text for his 'Si Hubbard.'" The song is in Sandburg's *The American Songbag*.

"The Big Shirt," another one of Bessie's old English ballads that she learned from Betsy Boblett, was unknown to me before I heard Bessie sing it, and I never found it in print. As I tape-recorded Bessie singing this long and slightly bawdy ballad about two lovers who get into a big shirt and then can't get out again, Bessie had Jimmie and me laughing at the predicament of Jack and Kate! Possibly an early broadside ballad, "The Big Shirt" became a favorite of mine and a standard part of my performance repertoire.

After I sang "The Big Shirt" at Indiana University in the late 1960s, Stith Thompson, the eminent folktale authority there, told me that the plot had been used by Boccaccio. According to Claude Simpson, rumors of similar songs have been since reported from the Bahamas and Canada.

Bessie's "Big Shirt" actually led to my meeting her in the first place. I had been booked to give a program at Ohio University for school music teachers by Dr. Edith Keller, music supervisor in the Ohio Department of Education. Edith (who had been an Ohio Wesleyan classmate of my mother, Fanny Laylin) was a wonderful help to me, since she was familiar with all of the state's counties, restaurants, hotels, and so on and arranged appearances for me at schools, historical societies, and social clubs—even at times accompanying me to the events as introducer.

The music teachers' group was a most receptive audience. Afterward, a sweet-faced, white-haired lady asked me if I'd ever heard of a song called "The Big Shirt." When the answer was negative, she said, "Just come over to Vigo and my mother will sing it for you." Her mother was Bessie Weinrich.

The Miller's Will

There was an old man in York did dwell.
He had three sons, and he loved them well.
This old man got very ill.
He thought it was time to make his will.
Sing rye, fodder, and hay.

He called up his oldest son,
Saying, "Sonny, oh sonny, my race is run.
To you the mill I will leave.
Pray, tell me the toll you mean to have."
Sing rye, fodder, and hay.

"Oh father, oh father, my name is Jack.
Of every bushel, I'll have a peck.
Of every grist that I do grind,
For such a fine living no man can find."
Sing rye, fodder, and hay.

"Oh sonny, oh sonny, as this won't do,
Since you won't do as I have done,
To you this mill I will not give;
For by such toll no man can live."
Sing rye, fodder, and hay.

He called up his second son,
"Oh, sonny, oh sonny, my race is run.
To you the mill I will give.
Pray, tell me the toll you mean to have."
Sing rye, fodder, and hay.

"Oh, father, oh father, my name is Ralph.
Of every bushel, I'll have a half.
Of every grist that I do grind,
For such a fine living no man can find."
Sing rye, fodder, and hay.

"Oh, sonny, oh sonny, as this won't do,
Since you won't do as I have done,
To you the mill I will not give;
For by such toll no man can live."
Sing rye, fodder, and hay.

He called up his youngest son,
"Oh, sonny, oh sonny, my race is run.
To you the mill I will give.
Pray, tell me the toll you mean to have."
Sing rye, fodder, and hay.

"Oh father, oh father, your darling boy,
In stealing corn is all my joy.
I'll steal the corn and swear to the sack,
And lick the boy when he comes back."
Sing rye, fodder, and hay.

"Oh, sonny, oh sonny, as this will do,
Since you will do as I have done,
The mill is yours!" the old man cried,
And shut his damned old eyes and died.
Sing rye, fodder, and hay.

The old man's dead and in his grave.
The greedy worms his flesh has craved.
But where he's gone, no one can tell.
But I suppose he's gone to Hell.
Sing rye, fodder, and hay.

The Fox

The fox went out in a hungry plight.
He begged the moon to give him light,
For he had many miles to trot that night
Before he could reach his den-oh,
Den-oh, den-oh.
For he had many miles to trot that night
Before he could reach his den, oh!

First he came to the farmer's yard.
The ducks and geese they thought it hard
That their nerves should be shaken and their
    rest be marred
By a visit of Mister Fox-oh,
Fox-oh, Fox-oh.
That their nerves should be shaken and their
    rest be marred
By a visit of Mister Fox-oh!

He took the gray goose by the sleeve,
And said, "Madam Goose, now by your leave,
I'll carry you off without reprieve
And take you home to my den-oh,
Den-oh, den-oh.
I'll carry you off without reprieve
And take you home to my den-oh."

He took the black duck by the neck
And strapped her up across his back.
And the old black duck went:
"Quack, quack, quack!"
And her legs hang dangling down, oh,
Down, oh, down, oh.
And the old black duck went:
"Quack, quack, quack!"
And her legs hang dangling down, oh.

Old Mother Slipper-Slapper jumped out of bed,
And out of the window she popped her head,
Saying, "John, John, John, the gray goose is gone
And the fox is off to his den-oh,
Den, oh, den, oh.
John, John, John, the gray goose is gone
And the fox is off to his den-oh."

John went up to the top of the hill,
And he blew a blast both loud and shrill.
"Oh, that's very pretty music,
Still, I'd rather be to my den-oh,
Den-oh, den-oh.
Oh, that's very pretty music,
Still, I'd rather be to my den-oh."

The fox got home to his hungry wife.
They did very well without fork and knife.
They never ate a better duck in all their life,
And the little ones picked the bones-oh,
Bones-oh, bones-oh.
They never ate a better duck in all their life,
And the little ones picked the bones-oh!

States and Capitals
The state of Maine, Augustie,
On the Kennebec River.
The state of Maine, Augustie,
On the Kennebec River.

Vermont, Montpelier,
On the Onion River.
Vermont, Montpelier,
On the Onion River.

Massachusetts, Boston,
On the Boston Harbor.
Massachusetts, Boston,
On the Boston Harbor.

New Hampshire, Concord,
On the Merrimac River.
New Hampshire, Concord,
On the Merrimac River.

Rhode Island has two capitals,
Providence and Newport.
Rhode Island has two capitals,
Providence and Newport.

Crockery Ware
Gentleman came a'courting here.
He courted a farmer's daughter dear.
A favor of her he did crave,
Was to come to her bed and to give him leave.
Tum a faddle laddle ling, tum a faddle laddle lay.
Faddle laddle linka dinka die-do lay.

This young lady strove to contrive
How her true love to deprive.
By the door she set a chair
And by the door put crockery ware.
Tum a faddle laddle ling, tum a faddle laddle lay.
Faddle laddle linka dinka die-do lay.

This young man rose all in the dark,
Thinking to get to his sweetheart.
He missed his way, I vow and declare,
And he broke his shins on the crockery ware.

Tum a faddle laddle ling, tum a faddle laddle lay.
Faddle laddle linka dinka die-do lay.

The old woman rose all in a fright.
Suddenly she called for a light,
Saying, "Who is here and who is there,
And who's broke all of my crockery ware?"
Tum a faddle laddle ling, tum a faddle laddle lay.
Faddle laddle linka dinka die-do lay.

This young lady lay laughing at the joke.
See how well her scheme did work.
Saying, "Oh my Jess, I caught you there—
You and Ma'am and the crockery ware."
Tum a faddle laddle ling, tum a faddle laddle lay.
Faddle laddle linka dinka die-do lay.

"Old woman, old woman, don't be so surprised.
I had an occasion for to arise.
I missed my way, I vow and declare,
And I broke my shins on the crockery ware."
Tum a faddle laddle ling, tum a faddle laddle lay.
Faddle laddle linka dinka die-do lay.

The old woman caught him by his lugs.
She gave him some unhappy chugs.
Saying, "I'll pull your hair, I vow and declare,
If you break any more of my crockery ware."
Tum a faddle laddle ling, tum a faddle laddle lay.
Faddle laddle linka dinka die-do lay.

Up the stairs he did go
With his heart both full of grief and woe.
Dressing his shins was all his care.
I'm sure he cursed the crockery ware.
Tum a faddle laddle ling, tum a faddle laddle lay.
Faddle laddle linka dinka die-do lay.

Come, all young folks, take warning of me,
Where e'er you are; where e'er you be.
Where e'er you are, pray take good care.
Don't break your shins on crockery ware!
Tum a faddle laddle ling, tum a faddle laddle lay.
Faddle laddle linka dinka die-do lay.

My Eyes Are Dim

(Spoken)
So the preacher got up. And he would always
read the song, and then the congregation would
sing. And he got up, and he got his Bible out, and
he said:

"My eyes are dim; I cannot see.
I left my specs at home."

(Sung)
"My eyes are dim; I cannot see.
I left my specs at home."

(Spoken)
"I did not mean for you to sing.
I left my specs at home."

(Sung)
"I did not mean for you to sing.
I left my specs at home."

(Spoken)
"What great big fools you all must be!
I left my specs at home."

(Sung)
"What great big fools you all must be!
I left my specs at home."

The Big Shirt
Jack and Kate sitting side by side,
Jack spied a shirt both large and wide.
"Oh Kate, oh Kate, come tell me true,
Does that big shirt belong to you?"
Raddle ring, raddle row. Faddle, raddle ring,
    raddle row.

"Oh, yes," says Kate, "it belongs to me."
"Oh, how extravagant you must be.
I wouldn't be afraid to take my oath
That that big shirt wouldn't hold us both!"
Raddle ring, raddle row. Faddle, raddle ring,
    raddle row.

"The Big Shirt" as sung by Bessie Weinrich. Notation by the author

"Now," says Kate, "if it wasn't for the shame,
  You and I would try that game."
"Good God!" says Jack, "What shame could
      there be
  When there's no one here but you and me?"
  Raddle ring, raddle row. Faddle, raddle ring,
      raddle row.

"Now," says Jack, "to begin,
  Both strip naked to the skin."
  When undressed and complete,
  Into the big shirt they did creep.
  Raddle ring, raddle row. Faddle, raddle ring,
      raddle row.

"Now," says Jack, "we've got in,
  How in the Devil will we get out again?
  This big shirt so much we pinch
  I cannot move myself one inch."
  Raddle ring, raddle row. Faddle, raddle ring,
      raddle row.

"There is a hook and pewter shelves
  We can reach and help ourselves.
  We can reach at our ease
  And can haul out by degrees."
  Raddle ring, raddle row. Faddle, raddle ring,
      raddle row.

They fastened a sleeve unto the hook.
A hearty pull or two they took.
The hook did break and let them fall.
Down come pewter shelves and all.
  Raddle ring, raddle row. Faddle, raddle ring,
      raddle row.

They rattled and splattered all over the room,
Just like the old Devil himself had come.
It wakened the old man; the old woman
      likewise,
And filled their hearts with sad surprise.
  Raddle ring, raddle row. Faddle, raddle ring,
      raddle row.

"Married," said the old man, "you must be.
  Five thousand guineas I'll give to thee;
  Five thousand, and it's all for above.
  It's more for shame than it is for love."
  Raddle ring, raddle row. Faddle, raddle ring,
      raddle row.

Jack and Kate in wedlock bound,
  They often think of the holy gown.
  When at home by themselves
  They laugh and talk of the pewter shelves.
  Raddle ring, raddle row. Faddle, raddle ring,
      raddle row.

Faye Wemmer with the author in Columbus, Ohio, early to mid-1950s. Photo by James W. Grimes

37 Faye Wemmer

Angels Sang Out the Sweet Story • There Is a Little Woman •
Babes in the Woods • Grandma Gruff

ATHENS COUNTY

FAYE WEMMER WAS just precious, marvelous, and ours was a long, long association.

Born in Athens County just over the Morgan County line, Faye learned some of her songs from her mother, and some she learned in school. She lived in the south end of Columbus with her husband, Jess, in a close-knit family with lots of children and grandchildren around, lots of singing and carrying on. In a letter to me that included lyrics of some of her songs, she wrote: "I'll write down the others you want whenever it gets quiet enough around here to be able to think."

The Wemmers had a summer place in Athens County at Burr Oak Lake near Faye's birthplace, where Jimmie and I and the kids also enjoyed visiting. We had lots of good times down there. And I got a lot of good leads—including Amanda Hook, to whom Faye introduced me after I performed one summer at a homecoming in nearby Jacksonville.

Faye contributed forty-eight items to my taped collection—including songs, hymns, recitations, and riddles. Her songs from her native Athens County, Ohio, included Child ballads, Civil War songs, a temperance song, and some songs on which I could not find information. Those included her simple, lyric, and lovely nativity, "Angels Sang Out the Sweet Story," which I called "Faye's Christmas Song."

Some of Faye's versions of traditional songs became standards in my repertoire, such as "There Is a Little Woman" and "Babes in the Woods" as well as "Grandma Gruff," with its whistling refrain.

Faye loved to sing, and her whole family was musical. Once when her brother-in-law, George Wemmer, and his family were visiting from out of town, Jimmie and I hosted the Wemmer clan with a buffet supper at our home and invited other Folklore Society members. Our musical entertainment that evening included George Wemmer playing violin; Jess Wemmer, harmonica; W. E. Lunsford, mandolin; me on dulcimer; and two of Faye's daughters, Verna on piano and Wilma on guitar.

As an active member of the Ohio Folklore Society in Columbus, Faye would call me once or twice a week with new ideas, and she was always sending the Grimes family texts of jokes or birthday cards—or if somebody was in the hospital, there was always a note or something. We were just really involved.

She was a close friend, too, of other Ohio Folklore Society members and contributors to my collection, like Ellie Flack and Dolly Church. When Dolly became terminally ill with cancer and did not want to be in the hospital, Faye's care enabled Dolly to spend her final days at home.

Faye died in 1959 at age fifty-eight. Her funeral was held at Concord Union Church in a beautiful grove of trees not far from Burr Oak Lake. Just a few weeks earlier, she had told me it was a place she wanted me to see.

I was asked by the family to sing an old hymn at the funeral that Faye had requested, "We'll Never Say Good-bye." I didn't know the tune to this particular hymn, but was able to get it over the phone from Ellie Flack. The chorus goes like this:

> We'll never say good-bye in Heaven
> We'll never say good-bye.
> For in that land of joy and singing,
> We'll never say good-bye.

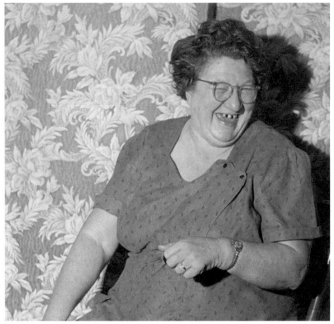

Faye Wemmer in Columbus, Ohio, early to mid-1950s.
Photo by James W. Grimes

Angels Sang Out the Sweet Story
Once in a manger lowly, hundreds of years ago,
A little babe so holy came to this world below.
Near was a crowded city, Bethlehem dark and cold.
It was a sight for pity. Chill was the night and cold.

Chorus:
Angels sang out the sweet story.
Fear not, for lo, this morn,
Jesus the Christ of glory,
A little babe was born.

Joseph and Mary, weary, no one would take them in,
Slept in a manger dreary nigh to a crowded inn.
Out on the hillside lowly shepherds beheld the sight,
For all the skies were lighted on that December night.
Chorus

Far from the east three strangers, led by the star their way,
Kept safely from great danger, seeking the Christ, they say,
Came to the manger lowly,
bringing their gifts of love,
Worshipped the babe so holy,
gift from the world above.
Chorus

There Is a Little Woman

There is a little woman that I've heard tell.
She went to market her eggs to sell.
She went to market all on market day,
And fell asleep on the king's highway.

Along came a peddler whose name was Stout.
He cut her petticoats all about.
He cut her petticoats off to her knees,
And this little woman began to freeze.

When this little woman began to wake,
She began to shiver, and she began to shake.
She began to wander, and she began to cry,
"Oh, lawka mercy on me, it can't be none of I.

"But if it be I, as I suppose it be,
I have a little dog at home. He'll know me.
And if it be I, he'll wag his little tail.
And if it be not I, he'll bark and he'll wail."

So home went the little woman all in the dark.
Up jumped the little dog, and he began to bark.
He began to bark, and she began to cry,
"Oh, lawka mercy on me, it can't be none of I."

Babes in the Woods

My dears, don't you know, a long time ago
Two poor little babes, their names I don't know,
Were stolen away one bright summer day
And left in the woods, I've heard people say.

The night then came on, and sad was their plight.
The sun a'goin' down,
and the moon gave no light.
They sobbed and they sighed
and they bitterly cried.
And the poor little things just lay down and died.

Then after they were dead, the robins so red
Carried strawberry leaves and over them spread.
And all the day long they would sing them a song.
Poor babes in the woods, poor babes in the woods.

Grandma Gruff

Grandma Gruff says a curious thing:
"Boys may whistle but girls must sing."
That's just what I heard her say.
'Twas no longer than yesterday.

Chorus:
Boys may whistle
[la la la la la or whistle]
Girls must sing,
Tra la la la la la la.
Boys may whistle
But girls must sing,
Tra la la la la la la la la la.

I asked father the reason why
Girls couldn't whistle as well as I.
Said he, "The reason the girls must sing
Is because they're a singular thing."
Chorus

Grandma Gruff says, "It would not do."
Gives us a very good reason, too.
Whistling girls and crowing hens
Always come to some bad end.
Chorus

38 Bird O. White and Anne White

Three Jolly Hunters

HOCKING COUNTY

BORN INTO A Hocking County settler family, Bird and Anne White were in their eighties when I tape-recorded them in 1958 at their home in Logan. The sisters sang several wonderful old English songs they learned from their mother, whose grandmother was Nancy Cantwell McBroom—a member of the Cantwell family who owned land that included Cantwell Cliffs and Rock House, now in Hocking Hills State Park.

Their songs included "Barb'ry Allen," "In Good Old Colony Times" (also known as "The Three Rogues"), and an extremely interesting old ballad, for which I could find no published reference, that begins, "As I was sailing down the main, I spied a ship coming down from Spain." It tells the story of a young woman who dies of love after learning from the ship's captain that her "sweet Willie" has drowned.

Another of their songs, "Three Jolly Hunters," is one that scholars have traced back to Shakespearean times. It has nonsensical lyrics about three hunters and the animals they encounter. The sisters remembered singing it—and also making up more verses about different animals—when they were "little bits of children."

The White sisters also gave me important lore related to the local murder ballad "Terrell," a song widely traditional in southeast Ohio that I had collected from Amanda Hook. When they were little girls, their father served as a court recorder at the trial of Bill Terrell for killing the Weldon family in 1878 in Gore, a town near Logan. The sisters said that many people thought Terrell might be innocent, or that others were involved, but circumstantial evidence was much against him.

Three Jolly Hunters

Oh, there were three jolly hunters,
And a'hunting they would go
With a rabbit dog, a pointer dog,
A setter dog also.
Lookee there now, lookee there now,
With a rabbit dog, a pointer dog,
A setter dog also.
Lookee there now.

So they roved and they rallied,
And the first thing they did find
Was a pig in a pen,
And that's the biggest kind.
Lookee there now, lookee there now,
Was a pig in a pen,
And that's the biggest kind.
Lookee there now.

Oh, the first said it was a pig,
And the second said, "Nay."
And the third said it was an elephant
With his trunk the other way.
Lookee there now, lookee there now,
And the third said it was an elephant
With his trunk the other way.
Lookee there now.

So they roved and they rallied,
And the next thing they did find
Was a sheep in the pen,
And that's the biggest kind.
Lookee there now, lookee there now,
Was a sheep in the pen,
And that's the biggest kind.
Lookee there now.

Oh, the first said it was a sheep,
And the second said, "Nay."
And the third said it was a bear
With his hair turned gray.
Lookee there now, lookee there now,
And the third said it was a bear
With his hair turned gray.
Lookee there now.

Then they roved and they rallied,
And the last thing they did find
Was an owl in the cedar tree,
And that's the biggest kind.
Lookee there now, lookee there now,
Was an owl in the cedar tree,
And that's the biggest kind.
Lookee there now.

Oh, the first said it was an owl,
And the second said, "Nay."
And the third said it was the devil,
And they all ran away.
Lookee there now.

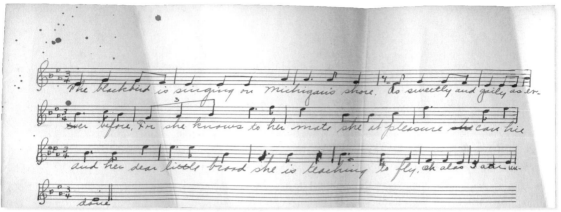

"Logan's Lament" notation by Anne Rayner Wilson

39 **Anne Rayner Wilson**

Logan's Lament

MIAMI COUNTY

MIAMI COUNTY IN west-central Ohio was one of the last centers of Native American life in Ohio— which may be one of the reasons that the ballad "Logan's Lament" was remembered so long there.

"Logan's Lament" tells the sad story in song of one of the causes of Lord Dunmore's War in the "Ohio Country" in 1774: the cold-blooded murder by renegade whites of the family of Mingo Chief Logan, a Moravian Christian, who had previously been a neutral peacemaker. Chief Logan "dug up the hatchet" when he heard of the massacre. He is said to have taken at least thirty scalps that summer and was raiding in Virginia at the time of the Battle of Point Pleasant, also commemorated in ballad.

Following the Battle of Point Pleasant, Logan refused to join the peace negotiations at Dunmore's Camp Charlotte on the Pickaway Plains, in what is now Pickaway County, Ohio. Tradition has it that Logan stated his grievances to Dunmore's envoy while standing under a large elm tree that later became known as "Logan's Elm." Logan concluded:

"Who is there left to mourn for Logan? Not one."

This "speech" was translated and spread throughout the East, partially by Thomas Jefferson, who admired its eloquence. Later poems based on it were printed in grammar school books—including the widely used *Sander's Fourth Reader,* published in Cincinnati in 1844—and featured in "literaries" of the period.

I tape-recorded Anne Rayner Wilson singing "Logan's Lament" in 1954 at her home in Piqua in Miami County. She sang it for me as it was sung in her childhood home when her family gathered in the evenings to sing, with her father playing on "a little" French harp.

Her father, J. A. Rayner, who was a Miami County historian, had learned it from his mother, Catherine Barrett Rayner, who grew up in the 1840s in Lebanon, Ohio. She had written down the words— probably when she was a girl.

Like her father, Mrs. Wilson had done considerable research on pioneer life and the folklore of Miami County. She also maintained the family's interest in Native Americans through her involvement in missionary work and schools in the West that included descendants of Native Americans from Miami County. The Rayner family is responsible for the preservation of "Logan's Lament" kept at the Ohio Historical Society in Columbus. Before his death in 1929, J. A. Rayner sent the society the words to the song; Mrs. Wilson later sent the tune.

It was Mrs. Wilson's impression that "Logan's Lament" had actually been composed and sung by Logan. She was not able to tell me what the word "Gehale" means in the last verse of the song, so at first I concluded that it was an added white romanticization. But Dr. August C. Mahr, authority on Ohio Native Americans and their language, later told me that "Gehale" might have had an authentic derivation, being similar to "kehelle," a phrase meaning "The one who speaks," used at the end of formal Delaware (not Mingo) orations.

A plaque five miles south of Circleville in Pickaway County today marks the former site of "Logan's Elm," supposedly nearly four hundred years old when it died in 1964 despite its careful preservation as a living historic relic. The Ohio state seal, with its background of Chillicothe's Mount Logan, is another reminder of Chief Logan.

Logan's Lament

The blackbird is singing on Michigan's shore
As sweetly and gaily as ever before.
For she knows to her mate she at pleasure can hie,
And her dear little brood she is teaching to fly.
Oh, alas, I am undone!

Each bird and each beast are as blest in degree.
All nature is cheerful and happy but me.
I will go to my tent and lie down in despair.
I will paint me with black and I'll sever my hair.
Oh, alas, I am undone!

I will sit on the shore where the hurricane blows
And reveal to the God of the tempest my woes.
I will weep for a season on bitterness fed,
For my kindred have gone to the hills of the dead.
Oh, alas, I am undone!

But they died not by hunger or lingering decay.
The steel of the white man hath swept them away.
The snakeskin that once I so sacredly wore
I will toss with disdain to the storm-beaten shore.
Oh, alas, I am undone!

They came to my cabin when heaven was black.
I heard not their coming, and I knew not their track.
But I saw by the light of their blazing fusees
They were people engendered beyond the big seas.
Oh, alas, I am undone!

I will dig up my hatchet and bend my oak bow.
By night and by day I will follow the foe.
No lake shall impede me, nor mountains nor snow.
Their blood can alone give my spirit repose.
Oh, alas, I am undone!

My wife and my children! Oh, spare me the tale,
For who is there left that is kin to Gehale?
My wife and my children! Oh, spare me the tale,
For who is there left that is kin to Gehale?
Oh, alas, I am undone!

40 Okey Wood and the Okey Wood Dulcimer

Dulcimer Playing and Erin's Green Shore

Dulcimer made by Okey Wood. Photo by David A. Kay

MEIGS
COUNTY

I FOUND OKEY WOOD living up Leading Creek in a pretty place in the hills outside Middleport, on the Ohio River. His roots were in West Virginia—which you could see right across the river. We were introduced thanks to my friend and contributor, Dolly Church, who lived in Columbus but spent her summers in her native Meigs County, where she "beat the bushes" for me.

Born in 1893, Okey Wood played a fine, large dulcimer he designed and made himself. To play it, he used a pick and crossfretted using his thumb, having lost the four fingers of his left hand in World War I. Okey's dulcimer was an extremely beautiful instrument of spruce and black walnut with six strings, a wide fretboard, a wide bout, and mechanical worm tuners—and an unusual shape and pretty sound holes. He made it when he was a young man living in his native Nicholas County, West Virginia, in about 1922. He recalled seeing a number of dulcimers in West Virginia, and said he knew a man in Greenbrier County who played a long, thin dulcimer with a bow.

I was so intrigued by Okey's dulcimer that about a year later, I got up the nerve to ask if there was any chance he might consider parting with it or making a new one patterned after it for me. He said he would sell it to me, and that he would make himself a better one. I bought the dulcimer, and I traced a pattern and left it with him, but I don't know if he ever made another.

Okey also sang ballads he said he had learned from his grandparents, like "Erin's Green Shore." Other songs I taped Okey singing were the murder ballads "Pearl Bryan" and "Naoma Wise," both with good tune and full text, as well as an interesting ballad about an Indian battle he thought had taken place in West Virginia, "We Walked across the Mountains to the Head of Williams River." He sang unaccompanied, and was quite a good ballad singer, although he said he rarely ever sang for friends or neighbors.

"Just once in a while, I'll be out on the porch, me and the woman . . . and be a little lonesome, or something . . . I might sing a song or two."

Erin's Green Shore

One evening for pleasure I rambled,
On the banks of a clear purling stream,
I set down on a hedge of trimmed roses,
And so softly I fell into a dream.

I dreamed that I seen a fair damsel,
Whose equal I'd ne'er seen before.
She seemed to mourn for the wrongs of her country,
As she roamed along the Erin green shore.

So, quickly I rose and addressed her,
"My jewel, come tell me your name,
In this country you know I'm a stranger,
Or I never would have acted so plain."

"I'm a daughter of Daniel O'Cornwell,
Quite lately from England sailed o'er.
I have come here to wake up my brother,
Who slumbered on the Erin green shore."

Her cheeks was like two blooming roses,
Her teeth of an ivory white,
And her eyes shone like two sparkling diamonds,
Or the stars on a cold winter night.

With the tenderest of joy I awoken,
And I found it was only a dream,
That this beautiful damsel had vanished,
And I longed to be a'slumbering again.

Yes, the beautiful damsel had vanished,
And I knew I couldn't see her no more.
May the angels of light, light her pathway,
As she roams along the Erin green shore.

CD Selections from the Anne Grimes Collection

1. "The Homestead Strike"—Reuben Allen (vocal, guitar); Zanesville, Ohio; 1953
2. "The Death of the Devil"—Bertha Bacon (vocal); Columbus, Ohio; 1956
3. "Seafaring Man"—Sarah Basham/Bertha Basham Wright (vocal); Columbus, Ohio; 1957
4. "Ohio Guards"—Henry Lawrence Beecher (vocal); Mt. Vernon, Ohio; 1953
5. "Lady and Laddie"—John Bodiker (vocal); Columbus, Ohio; 1957
6. "Gypsy Davey"—John Bodiker (vocal); Columbus, Ohio; 1957
7. "Spinning Wheel Riddle/Double Talk or Tricky Talk"—Dolleah Church (spoken); Columbus, Ohio; 1954
8. "The Pious Little Men"—sung and recorded by Walter W. Dixon; Rochester, New York; 1955
9. "Golden Slippers"—Ken Ward (dulcimer); Bidwell, Ohio; 1955
10. "The Liar's Song"—Ken Ward (vocal); Bidwell, Ohio; 1955
11. "The Jolly Scotch Robbers"—Blanche Wilson Fullen (vocal); Columbus, Ohio; 1957
12. "Our Goodman"—Bob Gibson (vocal, guitar); Columbus, Ohio; ca. early 1950s
13. "Watermelon Smiling on the Vine"/"There's a Beautiful Home"—Brodie F. Halley (dulcimer / vocal, dulcimer); Gallipolis, Ohio; 1954
14. "Dandoo"—Perry Harper (vocal); Ray, Ohio; 1955
15. "John Funston"—Anne Grimes (vocal, dulcimer); place and date unknown
16. "Cottage Hill" (excerpt)—Donald Langstaff (vocal); Toboso, Ohio; 1954
17. "The Farmer's Curst Wife"—Donald Langstaff (vocal); Toboso, Ohio; 1954
18. "Hush, My Babe"—Anne Grimes (vocal, dulcimer); recorded at Mills College, Oakland, California; 1970
19. "A Bonny Lass, a Happy Lass"—Bascom Lamar Lunsford (vocal, banjo); Columbus, Ohio; 1958
20. "Turkey in the Straw"—W. E. Lunsford (dulcimer); Columbus, Ohio; date unknown
21. "When the Roll Is Called Up Yonder"—Jane Jones McNerlin (dulcimer); Oak Hill, Ohio; 1953
22. "Hangman"—May Kennedy McCord (vocal, guitar); St. Louis, Missouri; 1953
23. "I Am a Soldier of Pancho Villa"—Jenny Wells Vincent (vocal, guitar); St. Louis, Missouri; 1953
24. "Jefferson and Liberty"—Pete Seeger (vocal, banjo); St. Louis, Missouri; 1953
25. "My Station's Gonna Be Changed"—Neva Randolph (vocal); Murray City, Ohio; 1953
26. "Rarden Wreck"—Babe Reno/Arbannah Reno (vocal, banjo); Piketon, Ohio; 1953
27. "Luck Is the Residue of Design" (excerpt)—Branch Rickey (spoken); Columbus, Ohio; 1954
28. "Record Makers"—Carl Sandburg (vocal, guitar); Columbus, Ohio; 1953
29. "My Eyes Are Dim"—Bessie Weinrich (vocal); Vigo, Ohio; 1954
30. "The Big Shirt"—Bessie Weinrich (vocal); Vigo, Ohio; 1953
31. "There Is a Little Woman"—Faye Wemmer (vocal); Columbus, Ohio; 1953
32. "Sally Goodin'" and untitled dulcimer piece—Okey Wood (dulcimer); Middleport, Ohio; ca. 1955
33. "Erin's Green Shore"—Okey Wood (vocal); Middleport, Ohio; ca. 1955

(left) The Okey Wood dulcimer. 1987 photo by Julie Elman

The CD included with this book represents a small sample of the some one thousand items that were tape-recorded by Anne Grimes. Her original tape recordings are housed at the American Folklife Center at the Library of Congress, Anne Grimes Collection, AFC 1996/003. A duplicate set of most of these tapes, along with some additional materials (including the original recording of Anne Grimes singing "Hush, My Babe"), is at the Ohio Historical Society, Anne Grimes Collection, AV201. For CD production information and credits, see Editors' Acknowledgments.

Editors' Notes

Traditional or folk music generally describes music "handed down" orally within a family or community for several generations. For the most part, Anne Grimes limited her collection to items that had been passed down in Ohio families through at least two generations. Exceptions included songs composed in the folk tradition like those of the composer Dan Emmett from Mt. Vernon, Ohio, or songs moving into the folk tradition like "The Ballad of Rodger Young," a ballad by Frank Loesser that Anne Grimes sang about a soldier from Tiffin, Ohio, who died in World War II.

The Child ballads that Anne Grimes collected are indicated throughout the book with their identification numbers as categorized by the Harvard scholar Francis James Child (1825–1896) in his classic *The English and Scottish Popular Ballads.* Anne Grimes describes their significance in her first mention of a Child ballad "find" in the chapter on Bertha Bacon, who sang "Lord Lovel" (Child #75).

Besides the Child ballads and bawdy material mentioned in the introduction, the other British survivals especially prized by Anne Grimes were the broadside ballads she found still being sung in Ohio in living tradition. Broadsides or "stall" ballads were products of early printing presses, published on single sheets of paper (broadsides) that were hawked in public places. Popular from the fifteenth through the nineteenth century, the British broadside ballads usually lacked musical notation. The tune was sometimes described under the title or sometimes sung by the vendor. References to broadsides are found related to the chapters on Amanda Hook, Lottie Leas, and Bessie Weinrich.

For more information on traditional music as passed down in Anne Grimes's own family, see the chapter on her mother, Fanny Hagerman Laylin.

Abbreviations

LAS refers to *A Catalogue of Pre-Revival Appalachian Dulcimers* by L. Allen Smith.

Randolph refers to the four-volume *Ozark Folksongs* by Vance Randolph.

Books cited by author's surname alone, or by author's name plus volume number, are listed with full publication details in the selected bibliography.

Frank Allen (18–20)

Frank Allen and his family were significant contributors to Rio Grande College, and biographical information on the Allens can be found in *Rio Grande: From Baptists and Bevo to the Bell Tower, 1876–2001,* by Abby Gail Goodnite and Ivan M. Tribe (Ashland, KY: Jesse Stuart Foundation, 2002).

Edna Ritchie Baker's remarks on Will Singleton (1860–1951) are quoted in LAS in Smith's introduction to "The Singleton Dulcimers (D56–D63)," a section of "Dulcimers with a Single Bout," page 73.

Although Anne Grimes wrote that Frank Allen neither owned nor played a dulcimer, some of the photographs of Allen taken by James Grimes show Allen holding a lap dulcimer. The editors think it must have belonged to Grimes.

The maker and date of the scantling in the Anne Grimes Collection are unknown. Smithsonian Collection Catalogue #1996.0276.06. LAS Type C: Dulcimers with Straight Sides, C10. Length: 1065 mm.

Reuben Allen (21–23)

"My Eyes Are Dim" features a parody of the practice of "lining out" hymns, congregational singing for which the leader offers a line of a hymn and the people in the congregation then take it up and follow. Popular in nineteenth-century churches (before the advent of printed tunes in hymnals), the practice continued into the twentieth century, especially in many black churches, where they were known as "Dr. Watts hymns," named after the English hymnologist, Isaac Watts.

For another version of "My Eyes Are Dim," see Bessie Weinrich.

Anne Grimes sang "The Underground Railroad" on her 1957 Folkways record, *Ohio State Ballads,* and the lyrics are published in her liner notes. The song is one of three she sang on the album related to the African American experience in early nineteenth-century Ohio. The other two are "My Darling Nelly Gray," a popular abolitionist song composed by Benjamin R. Hanby, and "My Station's Gonna Be Changed," which Grimes collected from another contributor featured in this book, Neva Randolph.

"The Underground Railroad" song was included in Joshua McCarty Simpson's *The Emancipation Car, Being an Original Composition of Anti-slavery Ballads Composed Exclusively for the Underground Railroad,* a rare songster (lyrics but no notation) published in Zanesville in 1854. Anne Grimes wrote that Simpson's tune must have been "O Susanna," since one of the choruses in the songster is:

O, Susannah, don't you
   cry for me.
I'm going up to Canada
Where colored men are free.

In her Folkways album notes, Anne Grimes related some of the history of pre–Civil War conflicts in Ohio. Although it was an antislavery state, Ohio supported both local and federal laws that provided severe penalties for harboring escaped slaves. For decades before and during the Civil War, many towns in Ohio saw conflicts between proslavery and abolitionist factions, some of them quite violent. Many Ohioans defied the fugitive slave laws to help thousands of slaves make their way across the state to freedom in Canada through the Underground Railroad system. Anne Grimes's maternal family in Richland County was among them.

Anne Grimes's personal music library included rare early editions of books on African American music such as *Liberty Minstrel,* by George W. Clark (New York, 1845); *Slave Songs of the United States* (New York: A. Simpson and Co., 1867); *The Story of the Jubilee Singers; With Their Songs,* by J. B. T. Marsh (New York: S. W. Green's Son, 1883); *The Negro and His Songs,* by Howard W. Odum and Guy B. Johnson (Chapel Hill: University of North Carolina Press/Oxford University Press, 1925); *Singing Soldiers,* by John Jacob Niles, a folk scholar who served in the air force in World War I and collected songs sung by African American soldiers serving in France (New York: Charles Scribner's Sons, 1927); *John Henry, Tracking Down a Negro Legend,* by Guy B. Johnson (Chapel Hill: University of North Carolina Press, 1929); and *White and Negro Spirituals,* by George Pullen Jackson (New York: J. J. Augustin, 1943). For additional information on the Underground Railroad, Grimes in her Folkways album liner notes referred to *The Mysteries of Ohio's Underground Railroad,* by William H. Seibert (Columbus, Ohio: Long's College Book Co., 1951), and to J. M. Simpson's *The Emancipation Car* (Zanesville, Ohio: Edwin C. Church, 1854), property of the Ohio Historical Society Library.

Anne Grimes's research into songs related to the Underground Railroad included in the fall of 1953 correspondence with Dr. John Hope Franklin (1915–2009), who at the time was a professor at Howard University and a member of the NAACP Legal Defense Fund team that worked with Thurgood Marshall on *Brown v. Board of Education,* which ended legal segregation in public schools.

In her notes on "The Homestead Strike," Anne Grimes referred to information on the New Straitsville coal fire published in *The Ohio Guide,* compiled by workers of the Writers' Program of the Work Projects Administration (New York: Oxford University Press, 1940). She also referenced *Coal Dust on the Fiddle: Songs and Stories of the Bituminous Industry,* by George Korson (Philadelphia: University of Pennsylvania Press, 1943), which includes a song Korson tape-recorded in 1940, titled "The Homestead Strike," about a steel mill strike in 1892 in Homestead, Pennsylvania.

In his book on American workers and their customs, *Wobblies, Pile Butts, and Other Heroes: Laborlore Explorations* (Urbana: University of Illinois Press, 1993), Archie Green included Reuben Allen's account of the New Straitsville fire. On page 250, he also included the words of Reuben Allen's "Homestead Strike" as transcribed by Green from the tape recording in the Anne Grimes Collection at the Library of Congress. Green's transcription varies slightly from Grimes's. In the last line of the second stanza, Grimes transcribed the line "And the _____ men come running up," while Green transcribed it as "And the [. . .] come blowing up." Not included here is a third stanza that Grimes and Green as well as the editors had difficulty transcribing.

The New Straitsville underground mine fire is still burning today.

Bertha Bacon (24–26)

Other taped contributors in the Anne Grimes Collection who sang versions of "Lord Lovel" were Elizabeth Law ("Lord Ullen") and Amanda Hook ("Lord Lovel's Daughter").

The only printed reference Anne Grimes could find to "Death of the Devil" (as she always referred to the song although Bertha Bacon herself called it "The Devil") was five verses in Randolph 3 ("The Devil Came to My Door") similar but not identical to Bertha Bacon's.

Anne Grimes noted that "Johnny Sands" is found in Randolph 4. She also found it listed as a favorite of the Hutchinson family, the famous nineteenth-century singing group from New Hampshire who performed in the United States and abroad.

Sarah Basham and Bertha Basham Wright (27–30)

Anne Grimes sang "Lass of Roch Royal" on her 1957 Folkways record, *Ohio State Ballads.* Some disagreed with Grimes's identification of Mrs. Basham's song as a version of the Child ballad, "Lass of Roch Royal." Critics included Tristram P. Coffin (in a review published in the *Ohio Historical Quarterly* in 1958) and Annabel Morris Buchanan in a 1957 letter to Grimes. Both documents are in Grimes's files. Despite this criticism, Grimes maintained her position on the title. Another version of "Lass of Roch Royal" in Grimes's taped collection was sung by May Kennedy Mc-Cord. See "The National Folk Festival at St. Louis: May Kennedy McCord, Jenny Wells Vincent, Pete Seeger" in this book.

Anne Grimes's notes on "Seafaring Man" (also titled "The Silk Merchant's Daughter") state that Mrs. Basham's version strongly resembled the one found in Arthur Palmer Hudson, *Folksongs of Mississippi and Their Background* (Chapel Hill: University of North Carolina Press, 1936), and was similar in text to (but with a different tune than) the version in Alton C. Morris, *Folksongs of Florida* (Gainesville: University of Florida Press, 1950). She also found other references in Brewster, Brown 2, Cox, Greenleaf, Randolph 1, and Sharp 1. Grimes noted that verse 2 of John M. Bodiker's "The Little Gypsy" (Anne Grimes Collection: Tape 74-E1) is identical to the first verse of Mrs. Basham's "The Seafaring Man" and that Mary O. Eddy's version of "The Gypsy's Wedding Day" starts with a similar verse.

Anne Grimes in her notes on "It Rained a Mist" wrote that Wright's lyrics are similar to those found in the collections of Mary O. Eddy, Bruce R. Buckley, and Reed Smith, among others, with slight differences. Grimes gave permission to Bertrand Harris Bronson to publish the text and tune of Wright's "It Rained a Mist" in volume 3 of *The Traditional Tunes of the Child Ballads* (Princeton: Princeton University Press, 1966), where it appears under "#155 Sir Hugh, or, The Jew's Daughter."

John W. Beattie (31–33)
"The Ohio Canal" by John W. Beattie was published in 1951 in book 6 of *The American Singer,* a series of songbooks for children published by the American Book Company, edited by John W. Beattie, Josephine Wolverton, Grace V. Wilson, and Howard Hinga.

One of the last of the canal boat captains, Captain Pearl R. Nye collected folksongs, wrote songs, and performed at the National Folk Festival in 1938, 1942, and 1946. Born in 1872 on a boat captained by his father and docked in Chillicothe on the Ohio and Erie Canal, he died in 1950 in Akron, Ohio. Anne Grimes sang a verse of Captain Nye's "Canal Dance" at the National Folk Festival in St. Louis on May 16, 1952, which began, "Come all you jolly boatmen, let us have a dance. Take off your shoes and cuff up your pants."

John Beattie in his letter to Anne Grimes in 1952 acknowledged the help of Edith Keller, state director of music education, in his canal research that began with a tip from John Lomax (whose recordings of Captain Nye are in the John A. Lomax Collection, American Folklife Center, Library of Congress) on a boatman who might know songs. Edith Keller and Cloea Thomas, of the Ohio State University music education department, also recorded and collected Nye for the Pearl R. Nye Collection at the Ohio Historical Society. Cloea Thomas was the compiler and editor of *Scenes and Songs of the Ohio-Erie Canal, Collected and Recorded by Captain Pearl R. Nye,* published by the Ohio Historical Society in 1971. Coincidentally, Edith Keller was a close friend of Grimes's mother, Fanny Laylin; and Cloea Thomas had been one of Grimes's elementary school music teachers.

James W. Grimes took several photographs of Margaret O. Moody. One is included in *Library of Congress American Folklife Center: An Illustrated Guide,* published in 2004, which includes a companion CD on which Mrs. Moody sings "Unconstant Lover" from the Anne Grimes Collection.

Henry Lawrence Beecher (34–38)
Anne Grimes sang "Ohio Guards" on her 1957 Folkways record, *Ohio State Ballads.*

Besides "Robin Hood Rescuing Three Squires" (Child #140), another Child ballad that Henry Beecher contributed was "Gypsy Davey" ("The Gypsy Laddie," Child #200). He also sang a Child ballad parody, "Lord Lovel, He Stood at the St. Charles Hotel" (see Bertha Bacon, "Lord Lovel").

For more on Ken Ward's version of the "Liar's Song," see the section "Dulcerine Players of Southeastern Ohio" and editors' notes to it. Beecher's version consisted of one verse. The lyrics were:

> Saw a sparrow run a harrow, Jilla-flow, Jilla-flow.
> Saw a sparrow run a harrow, Jilla-flow, my Jo.
> Saw a sparrow run a harrow all around the parson's meadow.
> And we'll all slap jack and be happy here below.

In "Ohio Guards," the third line—"General Cowen's order says"—refers to Benjamin R. Cowen, adjutant-general of Ohio during the Civil War, who called out the Ohio National Guard in 1864 to be used as "One Hundred Days'" men for garrison and guard duty. Other states tried the plan to relieve the regulars, but none acted so promptly as Ohio, where within sixteen days some 35,982 men were put into federal service.

Clarence Laylin sang a fragment of "Battle of the Boiling Water" included in the Anne Grimes Collection Tape 49-A1.

John M. Bodiker (39–48)

In a handwritten note added to the typed catalogue of her collection, Anne Grimes wrote next to John Bodiker's name: "The best!"

At the Ohio Folklore Society spring meeting, April 7, 1973, Anne Grimes gave a talk with the working title "Medieval and Renaissance Reflections and Ballad Survivals in Ohio. In Memoriam: John M. Bodiker, a Major Ohio Folklore Contributor, May 16, 1878–March 1, 1973. Based on collection by Anne Grimes tape-recorded in Columbus: March 1957 to December 1972." Later, she called her lecture "Bodiker's Bawdy Buckeye Ballads—Or 'Ribalds' Sung behind Paulding County, Ohio Barns in the 1880's." An abstract of the talk was published in the *Journal of the Ohio Folklore Society,* new series, 2, no. 3 (Winter 1973): 46–47.

In her notes on John Bodiker, Anne Grimes credited Vance Randolph as one of the few pioneer collectors who recognized bawdy material, even though he could not get it published in his classic, four-volume *Ozark Folksongs* (Columbia: State Historical Society of Missouri, 1946–50). Randolph later was able to get some of his bawdy material published, including in *Pissing in the Snow and Other Ozark Folktales* (Urbana: University of Illinois Press, 1976), with a foreword by Frank A. Hoffman and dedicated to Gershon Legman.

Anne Grimes described "Lady and Laddie" as "unique." She also wrote that it was related in plot to (but completely different from and probably older than) "Johnny Sands" and "Eggs and Marrowbones."

As part of her research on "The Substitute," Anne Grimes corresponded with Kenneth Goldstein, the folklore authority and editor of her Folkways record, and Rae Korson, the head of the Archive of Folk Song of the Library of Congress. In her research notes, Grimes wrote that "Doo Me Ama," included in *Frontier Ballads* by Charles Finger, is nearest in plot to Bodiker's version.

Besides the ones presented here, Bodiker's bawdy ballads also included "The Bonny Black Hare," "Derby Ram," "I Went to a Barber," "Snap Poo," "There Was an Old Dutchman," "Adam and Eve Recitation" ("Little Piece of Whang"), "The Sea Crab" (fragment), "The Keyhole in the Door," "The Little Ball of Yarn," and "Way Down in Maine."

In her notes on "The Jealous Sister" ("The Two Sisters," Child #10), Anne Grimes wrote that sometimes the song was "played" or acted out while being sung, which may account for the "bow down" refrain.

Anne Grimes kept in her files a typed document sent to her by John Bodiker that he titled "The Folklore Festival at Nashville Tenn." In it, Bodiker describes his many activities at the National Folk Festival in 1959, including a breakfast meeting with Sarah Gertrude Knott and Jenny Wells Vincent. (See "The National Folk Festival at St. Louis: May Kennedy McCord, Jenny Wells Vincent, Pete Seeger.")

Paul Bogatay (49–50)

In her notes on Bogatay's version of the "The Sea Crab," Anne Grimes cited "The Bawdy Song . . . in Fact and in Print," by Gershon Legman (1917–1999). Legman claimed that "The Sea Crab" had "the longest unbroken genealogy of any bawdy song in English" and called the song one of Child's "most serious silent omissions." See *Explorations: Studies in Culture and Communication* 7 (March 1957): 13, edited by Edmund Carpenter and Marshall McLuhan; published by the University of Toronto.

Anne Grimes's notes on "The Sea Crab" also included references to *The Erotic Muse,* by Ed Cray (New York: Oak, 1969).

Dolleah Church (51–53)

"Abominable bee with its tail cut off": For similar wordplay, see William L. Utter's contribution at the end of the notes to William T. Utter below.

Ben Hayes, the longtime columnist for the *Columbus Citizen,* was a friend of Anne Grimes from her days as music critic at the *Columbus Citizen,* 1942–45. A student of local history, Hayes wrote about people of interest in the Ohio capital. His work includes a tribute to Dolly Church following her death in 1958, "Lest we forget . . . Mrs. Dolleah Church," an excerpt of which is quoted here in the text.

James M. Cox (54–55)

James Middleton Cox (1870–1957), three-time governor of Ohio, was the Democratic presidential candidate in 1920, with Franklin D. Roosevelt as his running mate. Raised on his father's farm near Dayton, Ohio, Cox was editor-publisher of the *Dayton Daily News* and founder of Cox Enterprises.

Jefferson Patterson (1891–1977) donated his family homestead, built by his great-grandfather, Col. Robert Patterson, to the city of Dayton in ceremonies that took place on November 20, 1953. Jefferson Patterson was the son of Frank Patterson, a founder with his elder son, John, of the National Cash Register Company.

Anne Grimes's notes on the Harding campaign song referenced its composer, Ohioan Ernest R. Ball. Grimes's singing of this song was tape-recorded by Ohio Wesleyan University when she included it as part of her acceptance speech at the Ohio Wesleyan University Alumni Association's Distinguished Achievement Award Ceremony in 1994.

See the editors' notes on Fanny Laylin for more information on Lewis Cass Laylin, the grandfather of Anne Grimes, who served as Ohio's Secretary of State and Speaker of the House in the state legislature and also as United States Assistant Secretary of the Interior under presidents Taft and Wilson.

Walter W. Dixon (56–57)
Anne Grimes's scholarly article "Possible Relationship between 'Jump Jim Crow' and Shaker Songs" was published in *Midwest Folklore* 3, no. 1 (1953): 47–57. Sources cited there by Grimes include Shaker hymnals and reminiscences of those who were neighbors of the Shakers, as well as the published works of Edward Deming Andrews (*The Gift to Be Simple: Songs, Dances and Rituals of the American Shakers,* 1940) and Caroline B. Piercy (*The Valley of God's Pleasure,* 1951). Grimes reviewed Piercy's *The Shaker Cook Book: Not by Bread Alone* in the *Ohio State Archaeological and Historical Quarterly* 63, no. 1 (January 1954): 83–85.

"Shakers Dance," a Shaker-related song to the tune of Dan Emmett's "Boatman's Dance," was collected (but not taped) by Anne Grimes in the early 1950s from Elizabeth Frost. "Shakers Dance" and the Shaker classic "Simple Gifts" were sung by Anne Grimes on collection tape AGM10.

Dulcerine Players of Southeastern Ohio: Bob White, Ken Ward, Lilly McGhee Ward Swick, Charles Ralston (58–62)
In an article by Anne Grimes published in the *Columbus Dispatch,* Sunday, March 27, 1955, she said that the word "dulcerine" instead of "dulcimer" was used to show the difference between the handmade, plucked instrument and the factory-made hammered dulcimer.

Anne Grimes wrote that John Wright was the earliest known maker of the type of dulcimer that she found in southeastern Ohio as played by Bob White, Ken Ward, Lilly Swick, Charles Ralston, and Ernest Russel. See also Arthur Tyler.

Anne Grimes's dulcimer collection includes three dulcimers with the same basic design as seen in the photographs of the Wards and White:

—The Tyler Dulcimer. Made in 1894 by Arthur Tyler of Columbus, modeled on a dulcimer brought to central Ohio from Vinton County. The Tyler Dulcimer shares the characteristics of those played by Bob White and Ken Ward. Smithsonian Collection Catalogue #1996.0276.23. LAS Type E: Dulcimers with Double Bouts, E46. Length: 912 mm. See also the section and editors' notes on Arthur Tyler.

—The Russel Dulcimer. Anne Grimes bought the dulcimer from Ernest Russel, a traditional dulcimer player and maker who also was working as a cemetery caretaker in Gallipolis in Gallia County when she met him. Grimes previously had not met any traditional players who had made dulcimers to sell, but Russel estimated that he had sold some one hundred of his dulcimers to people all over southeastern Ohio. A native of Meigs County, Russel told Grimes that he had known and played dulcimer with both George Butcher and Wib White. Like them—and Arthur Tyler—Russel referred to the instrument as "dulcerine." Smithsonian Collection Catalogue #1996.0276.24. LAS Type E: Dulcimers with a Double Bout, E47. Length: 839 mm.

—A dulcimer that Grimes identified only as being from Gallia County. It has painted stars above and below the sound holes. Smithsonian Collection Catalogue #1996.0276.22. LAS Type E: Dulcimers with a Double Bout, E45. Length 884 mm.

According to Anne Grimes's notes on "The Liar's Song," the song had been traced by the ballad-scholar George Lyman Kittredge ("Note on a Lying Song," *Journal of American Folklore* 39 [1926]: 196) to an early sixteenth-century English manuscript "commonplace book."

Anne Grimes noted that versions of "The Liar's Song" are included in the collections of Randolph 3 (as "Johnny Fool") and Hudson (as "Old Blind Drunk John"). Grimes also noted that a version of "Liar's Song" from Scottish tradition, "We're a Jolly Fu,'" was recorded by Ewan MacColl on *Scots Drinking Songs* (Riverside Records).

For another verse of "Liar's Song," see the section and editors' notes on Henry Lawrence Beecher. Beecher knew little of the song's history in his family, of English descent. In performance, Anne Grimes sang a collation of the Beecher and Ward versions of "Liar's Song."

Arthur Byrd Fields (63–64)
Anne Grimes sang Arthur Field's traditional version of "Christ in the Garden" on her 1957 Folkways record, *Ohio State Ballads.*

Anne Grimes also tape-recorded Fields reading from his family hymnbook its publication details: published by Arrowood Brothers, Wayne, West Virginia, 1854, by Edward W. Billups, "Clerk's Office, District of Ohio."

Anne Grimes cited the following references on "Christ in the Garden," in addition to Billups: *American Church Harp* (Cincinnati: W.W. Rinehart, 1850); George Pullen Jackson, *Down-East Spirituals and Others* (New York: J. J. Augustin, 1941); Helen Hartness Flanders and Marguerite Olney, *Ballads Migrant in New England* (New York: Farrar, Straus and Young, 1953); and *West Virginia Folklore* 5, no. 4 (Summer 1960), which has a similar condensed version of five verses, "Ballad of Christ in the Garden of Gethsemane."

Bill Fields, the nephew of Arthur Fields, contributed ten songs to the Anne Grimes Collection.

"Lining out." For a parody of this oral tradition where the minister delivers the text and the congregation sings in response, see the sections on Reuben Allen and Bessie Weinrich.

Ella Strawser Flack (65–67)
In her notes on "Pretty Nancy," Anne Grimes cited "Sweet William and Lovely Nancy" in *Devil's Ditties* by Jean Thomas and "William and Nancy" in Sharp 2. She also referred to Margaret O. Moody's singing of "Unconstant Lover" (Anne Grimes Collection: Tape 21–3).

Blanche Wilson Fullen (68–71)
In her notes on "The Cruel Mother," Anne Grimes cited versions by other collectors: Child, Davis, Eddy, Flanders and Olney, and Sharp 1. She found a similar version of "Jolly Scotch Robbers" in Gardner and Chickering's *Ballads and Songs of Southern Michigan* (1939), titled "The Three Scotch Robbers."

Bob Gibson (72–74)
"Our Goodman" sung by Bob Gibson, with guitar accompaniment, in the Anne Grimes Collection, is similar to the version recorded on Columbia Records in 1929 titled "Drunkard's Special," sung by Coley Jones, an African American musician from Dallas, Texas. Jones's version is included in volume 1 of *The Anthology of American Folk Music,* a six-album compilation of eighty-four American folk, blues, and country music recordings that were originally issued from 1927 to 1932. The anthology was released in 1952 by Folkways Records and re-released by Smithsonian Folkways in 1997.

In her notes on "Our Goodman," Anne Grimes referenced Sharp 1 and Cray ("Five Nights Drunk"). Cray's commentary on the song (in *The Erotic Muse: American Bawdy Songs,* 2nd ed., Urbana: Illini Books edition, University of Illinois Press, 1999) includes the following: "Joseph Hickerson of the Library of Congress's Archive of American Folk Song has suggested that

'Our Goodman' (Child #274) may well be the most popular of the English and Scottish popular ballads in oral tradition.... According to Hickerson, were not informants and collectors handicapped by modesty, printed texts and tunes would surpass in number the acknowledged leader, 'Barbara Allen' (Child #84)."

In addition to the versions of "Our Goodman" performed by Bob Gibson and Bill Fields, Anne Grimes tape-recorded fragments of the ballad from Sarah Basham and Bertha Basham Wright, John Bodiker, Elizabeth Law, and Mrs. Harry I. Lewis. Bronson includes the lyrics of the fragment sung by Elizabeth Law from the Anne Grimes Collection in his *The Singing Tradition of Child's Popular Ballads.* Bronson titled it "Came Home the Other Night" (from the first line). Born in 1872, Laws told Grimes that she learned most of her songs from her aunts and uncles in Jackson, Ohio.

Mary O. Eddy included a version of "Our Goodman" in *Ballads and Songs from Ohio* with references to other collections, including those by Barry, Cox, Davis, Hudson, and Sharp 1.

Besides "Our Goodman," other items sung by Bob Gibson on Tape 4 in the Anne Grimes Collection are "Molly Flanagan" (Roger Sprung version), "Talkin' Blues" (hear a chicken sneeze), "Mary Had a Wristwatch," "Consumptive Sara Jane," "OK, Lady, I'll Buy Your Goddamned Violets," "They're Moving Father's Grave to Build a Sewer," and "Who Ha' Ya Las' Nicht" (mock Scottish). Rose Gibson on Tape 4 also sang "Cats on the Rooftops."

Items contributed by Bob Gibson to Tape 97 in the Anne Grimes Collection include his banjo lesson, "Run Come See" (with Anne Grimes on harmony); one verse of "Hey Li Lee Lo"; "Jenny Jenkins"; "Hush, Little Baby" ("All My Trials"); "I'm Weary With Sorrow"; "Down By the Bay"; and "Katey Morey," which, Anne Grimes noted, Gibson had learned from Howard Bell in Lakewood, Ohio. Also present and recorded was Bob Gibson's friend, the folksinger Rowena (Rowena Reik), who sang "Uncle Reuben."

In her interview with Ellen Gibb, Anne Grimes spoke about attending a Bob Gibson concert at the Gate of Horn in Chicago in the 1950s, and the singing there of "St. Clair's Defeat," which was a song Grimes sang on her 1957 Folkways record, *Ohio State Ballads.*

In 1957, Rose Gibson wrote to Anne Grimes from Chicago that Bob was interested in doing an album from the songs Grimes had sung and taped for him, with Grimes doing the liner notes. Rose said in her letter that Bob had talked to Riverside about the idea but wanted

Grimes's reaction before going further. Rose also wrote:

> Both of us think your material is the greatest and we continually play the tape you made for Bob when we visited you some years ago and Bob says he must admit that he listens with a covetous ear. He certainly would be very proud to have the honor of being the first to record some of your songs.

A. B. Graham (75–76)

A. B. Graham's career as an educator included administrative positions at Ohio State University and at the U.S. Department of Agriculture, where he served for twenty-three years in Washington, D.C., before returning to Ohio. One of the originators of the 4-H Club movement, he founded the Boys' and Girls' Agricultural Clubs in 1902 when he was superintendent of Springfield (Ohio) Township schools. While at Ohio State, he helped plan for junior high schools in the United States. He remained a booster of rural education all his life, long after his "retirement" in 1938. He also was one of the first candid photographers in the United States, and a collection of his work on 3″ x 4″ glass plates has been preserved at the Ohio Historical Society.

A few months after taping Graham singing his "Hayes Campaign Song," Anne Grimes found the original printing of the song titled "Hayes' Band" at the Hayes Memorial Library and Museum in Fremont, Ohio, where she performed. The song was included in "Helmick's Republican Campaign Songbook" (Cincinnati: F. W. Helmick, 1876). Grimes obtained a copy from the library, which she sent to Graham.

Anne Grimes collected a longer version of "Three Jolly Welshmen," as "Three Jolly Hunters," from Bird O. White and Anne White. For more on the song, see the section and editors' notes on the White sisters.

Other guests at the May 1957 party included Bertha Bacon, Sarah Basham, John Bodiker, Ella Flack, Blanche Fullen, William Lunsford, Arthur Tyler, Faye Wemmer, and Bertha Basham Wright.

The Anne Grimes contributor files include a letter by A. B. Graham recounting the story of his life, typed at his request by John Bodiker, dated May 10, 1958. The letter relates in some detail Graham's early life on a mortgaged farm that ended in the winter of 1879 when a fire destroyed their farmhouse, killed his father, and severely burned and otherwise injured all family members.

Brodie Franklin Halley (77–79)

The location of the Halley dulcimer is unknown. Anne Grimes's notes indicate that Brodie Franklin Halley willed it to a daughter.

Perry Harper (80–83)

Perry Harper was one of seventeen contributors who taped versions of "Barbara Allen" for the Anne Grimes Collection. Others who sang versions of "House Carpenter" were John Bodiker, Fred High, Amanda Hook, Charlie Perry, Faye Wemmer, Roberta Whitacre, and Bertha Basham Wright. Those who contributed versions of "Dandoo" were Lillian Adams, John Bodiker, Mrs. Dudley Miller, and Faye Wemmer.

In her notes related to "The Nightingale" (also titled "One Morning in May"), Anne Grimes referenced Brown 3, Eddy, Laws, Randolph 1, Sandburg (*The American Songbag*), and Sharp 2.

Amanda Styers Hook (84–86)

The ballad "Terrell" tells the story of William V. Terrell, the man convicted of murdering the Weldon family in Hocking County, Ohio. Terrell died of consumption February 15, 1884, in the Ohio Penitentiary, according to *Historical Reminiscences of the Ohio Penitentiary from Its Erection in 1835 to the Present Time,* by J. H. Matthews, published by Charles M. Cott, Columbus, Ohio, 1884. Grimes spelled the title of the song several ways, including "Terrill," "Terrel," and according to its Hocking County pronunciation, "Turl."

Other taped contributors to the Anne Grimes Collection who sang "Terrell" and/or contributed lore about the murder of the Weldon family were Perry Harper, Zora Johnson, Ina Simmons, Roberta Whitacre, Anne and Bird O. White, W. W. Wilson, Marion Wood, and sisters Hannah Campbell and Alma Henderson.

Arthur Emerson Kieffer (87–90)

The lyrics for "John Funston" here are as sung by Anne Grimes. They differ only slightly from the lyrics sung by Arthur Kieffer. The tune is the same.

Burleigh Cartmell wrote to Anne Grimes about the murder of William Cartmell in a letter dated July 16, 1954.

In an August 1957 letter to Edna Buchanan, then national archivist for the National Federation of Music Clubs, Anne Grimes said that she had wanted to record "John Funston" for many reasons, including its rich lore and historical background. However, she said that Kenneth Goldstein, the producer of her Folkways record, thought it too long and complicated for recording purposes.

Donald Langstaff (91–94)

Anne Grimes sang "The Farmer's Curst Wife" on her 1957 Folkways record, *Ohio State Ballads.*

Anne Grimes collected four distinctly different full versions of "The Farmer's Curst Wife"—from Sarah Basham, John Bodiker, Donald Langstaff, and Bessie Weinrich.

A song similar to "Cottage Hill" was collected in northwestern Pennsylvania as a lumber camp song by John C. French and published as "Our Wandering Boy Tonight" in *Northern Minstrelsy of Pennsylvania* (Altoona Tribune Co., 1919), page 44, and in *Minstrelsy of Pennsylvania* (Newman F. McGirr, 1931), page 54, both compiled by Henry W. Shoemaker (1880–1958), a cofounder of the Pennsylvania Folklore Society who served from 1923 to 1930 as chairman of the Historical Commission of Pennsylvania. Grimes also cited Brown 3 ("The Wood Hauler"), Cox ("When I Was One-and-Twenty"), and the Lomaxes in *Our Singing Country* ("I Came to the Country in 1865"). She later taped John Bodiker singing a song similar to "Cottage Hill" that Bodiker called the "Coal Hauler."

A founding member of the Ohio Folklore Society in 1950, Dr. Tristram P. Coffin later joined the faculty of the University of Pennsylvania and served as secretary of the American Folklore Society.

Fanny Hagerman Laylin (95–101)
From 1940 to 1942, Anne Grimes produced a weekly music program on WOSU radio, arranging, writing program notes, and accompanying guest artists, as well as performing piano and vocal solos.

In the 1950s, Anne Grimes taperecorded her mother singing "There Was a Little Man" and two other children's songs: "Two Little Kittens" and "Mr. Duck and Mr. Turkey." Also present at this recording session was her father, Clarence Laylin, who sang a fragment of "Battle of the Boiling Water," a bawdy fraternity song, and joined in on the family's singing in three-part harmony of "God Moves in a Mysterious Way."

Anne Grimes's maternal grandmother, Adeline Hagerman (1856–1942) wrote a booklet in her later years, *A Short Narrative and Family Records*, in which she described in moving detail what life was like growing up on a farm in Richland County in the mid-nineteenth century, including how much music meant to her family—beginning with her maternal great-grandparents, Joseph and Elizabeth Dickens Ward.

Joseph and Elizabeth Dickens Ward were married in 1798 in Newton Solney, Derbyshire, England, where Elizabeth was born in 1777. She was a cousin of the father of Charles Dickens, the great English novelist. As a musician in Repton, England, Joseph Ward is described as

having a tenor voice of rare quality that gained him much attention outside his community, so that when Haydn's *Creation* was first given in London, Ward was selected to sing the tenor part of Gabriel. (Joseph Ward's copy of Haydn's oratorio was passed down in the family and given to Anne Grimes by her grandmother.)

The singing schools Joseph Ward established in Richland County following his arrival there in 1819 were still in existence during the childhood of his great-grand-daughter Adeline Hagerman in the mid-nineteenth century. She wrote: "A tradition in Weller Township handed down from Joseph Ward was that everyone should learn to read music by note, 'do, re, mi, fa, sol, la, ti, do.' So evening singing schools were held during the winter months in the schoolhouses just as my great grandfather Ward held them in the scattered log schoolhouses in the early days."

Family ties in Richland County for subsequent generations were strengthened when two Ward daughters married two Palmer brothers after they met on the ship coming over from England. As British music continued in the family, to this was added much local lore, such as that of the Underground Railway, in which the family took an active part.

Fanny Hagerman Laylin (1884–1968) married Clarence "Pete" Dewey Laylin (1882–1970) in 1909. The couple met in Norwalk, Huron County, Ohio, where their fathers were, respectively, minister and president of the Official Board of the Methodist church. After they were married, the Clarence Laylins moved to Columbus, where Fanny Laylin was active in many civic, church, and cultural activities. She was a trustee of Ohio Wesleyan University, her alma mater and—like her mother-in-law, Frances Laylin—was active in theater and other productions of Sorosis, a club organized in 1897 to stimulate intellectual development and promote good fellowship among Columbus women.

As an undergraduate at Ohio State University, Clarence Laylin was the playing conductor of the popular Mandolin Club. He became a prominent Columbus utilities and corporation lawyer and tax expert for the National Chambers of Commerce. He was also a professor of law at Ohio State, where he served as the athletic board chairman. He also served as president of the Columbus Philharmonic Orchestra Association. He was the author of historical publications and an honorary life member of the Ohio Historical Society. A president of the Ohio Council of Churches, he was given an honorary doctorate of laws by Ohio Wesleyan University for his service as a Methodist layman.

Clarence Laylin's family included early settlers of Ohio who took an active part in the development of the state. His father, Lewis Cass Laylin (1848–1923), was the United States Assistant Secretary of the Interior under presidents Taft and Wilson. A lawyer and distinguished orator, Lewis Cass Laylin was Speaker of the House in the state legislature, which he entered from Huron County, as well as Ohio's Secretary of State. His older brother, Theodore, was a leader in the early Ohio Grange.

Clarence Laylin's mother, Frances Dewey Laylin (1854–1935), was an early leader in women's social and political movements in Ohio. She also was active in musical and theatrical amateur circles. She served as president of the Columbus Federation of Women's Clubs and of Sorosis, for which she both performed in and directed Shakespearean productions. She was Ohio state regent of the Daughters of the American Revolution and an ardent member of the Order of Founders and Patriots of America and Colonial Dames societies. Her interest in genealogy and American history stemmed from the fact that the two branches of her family, Wolcott and Dewey, emigrated from England on the same ship and settled in Connecticut in 1630; Wolcotts and Deweys were prominent in colonial government and in the Revolution before migrating to Ohio's Firelands, where her father, John Dewey, in 1862 was appointed by President Lincoln as northeast Ohio district tax collector.

D. K. Wilgus counted "Methodist Pie" among a wide range of "spiritual, Gospel, and heart songs" for which "one can date 'origins' over a century and a half." (*Journal of American Folklore* 81, no. 322 [October–December, 1968]: 378.) Anne Grimes noted the song's presence in Randolph 2. She often sang the song in performance, including at a Richland County family reunion. Her comments on its history are from her file notes, where she also wrote: "An echo of Midwestern pioneer worship, as both spiritual Revival and relief of backwoods monotony, the song continued to be widely sung with lusty relish. Sometimes the chorus is: 'Baptist, Baptist is my belief.'"

In regard to "There Was a Little Man," Anne Grimes's 1951 edition of *The Oxford Dictionary of Nursery Rhymes,* edited by Iona and Peter Opie, offers this comment: "A fanciful explanation given by Kathleen Thomas in *The Real Personages of Mother Goose* is that Philip of Spain, Mary Tudor, and Sir Francis Drake are depicted."

In her notes on "Froggie Went A'Courting," Anne Grimes referenced Morris, Opie #175, Randolph 1, and Sharp 2; her taped contributors include Eliza Jane Carter, Austin D. Cruisie, Mrs. J. W. Haigler, Henry Jr. Linton, Joseph M. Markley, Lucille Ball Naylor, Mary L. Spinning, Bessie Weinrich, sisters Hannah Campbell and Alma Henderson, and brother and sister Edward Starr and Helen C. Sevitts. Grimes wrote that her version of the song was the one she had learned in her Richland County tradition, with additional Buckeye contributors' verses. For "Father Grumble," Grimes referenced Laws, Randolph 1, and Tolman and Eddy, "Traditional Texts and Tunes," *Journal of American Folklore* 35 (October–December 1922): 366. Taped contributors included General Custer Nicholas, Jessie Parrish, Edna Ross, and Bessie Weinrich.

The words here for "Froggie Went A'Courting" and "Father Grumble" are from combined tape-recorded performances by Anne Grimes, including her program at the Smithsonian Institution in 1997.

Lottie Leas (102–5)

Anne Grimes sang "St. Clair's Defeat" on her 1957 Folkways record, *Ohio State Ballads,* and the lyrics included here are from that record. In its accompanying booklet, she wrote about the history of the battle and about the ballad and its tune. She referred readers to these bibliographical items: Frazer E. Wilson's *Arthur St. Clair, Rugged Ruler of the Old Northwest: An Epic of the American Frontier;* Mary O. Eddy's *Ballads and Songs of Ohio; Hill Country Tunes,* by Samuel Preston Bayard; and *Folkways Ballads of the War of 1812,* sung by Wallace House with lute.

"St. Clair's Defeat" also was collected in Ohio by Mary O. Eddy, who included it in her book as "On the Eighth Day of November." However, in correspondence with Anne Grimes, Eddy acknowledged that her version was less complete and had a less satisfactory tune than the Darke County version collected by Grimes.

Frazer E. Wilson wrote Anne Grimes two long letters that include mention of the "marked musical talent" in the Woods family, the impact of St. Clair's defeat on later pioneers who settled the area, and the notation of the ballad by Lottie Leas, "who recorded it nicely" for his 1938 broadside. The broadside itself credits the notation to Lottie Leas' mother, Rebecca Woods Leas, as sung by her aunt, Anna Woods Turner. Grimes noted that despite Wilson's copyright on his broadside, the identical lyrics (without tune) of the Darke County version of the ballad could be found—"along with some wonderful eyewitness accounts of the bloody disaster"—in *Howe's History of Ohio,* first published in 1847.

After receiving "St. Clair's Defeat" in October 1951 from William T. Utter, Anne

Grimes started her research on the song that led to her meeting in Darke County, Ohio, with Lottie Leas. Grimes wrote in November 1951 to George Korson, an expert in Pennsylvania and miners' songs and lore, about information she had discovered in Korson's book *Pennsylvania Songs and Legends* in a chapter written by Jacob A. Evanson, "Folk Songs of an Industrial City." Evanson had quoted Henry M. Brackenridge's *Recollections of Persons and Places in the West*, published in 1834, on Loughey's singing at a Pittsburgh racetrack. Grimes corresponded with Dr. Evanson, who sent her further information. Besides Korson, Evanson, Wilson, and Eddy, Grimes also corresponded about the ballad with Rae Korson, who was then reference assistant in (and later head of) the Folklore Section of the Library of Congress.

Bascom Lamar Lunsford (106–7)
Anne Grimes's papers include several handwritten letters from Bascom Lamar Lunsford dated from 1952 to 1958, and her library includes a signed copy of his *30 and 1 Folksongs (From the Southern Mountains)*, compiled and arranged by Bascom Lamar Lunsford and Lamar Stringfield (New York: G. Fischer, 1929).

W. E. Lunsford and the John H. Lunsford Dulcimer (108–9)
Anne Grimes also collected a dulcimer version of "Turkey in the Straw" from Arthur D. Tyler.

The John H. Lunsford Dulcimer is Smithsonian Institution Catalog #1996.0276.20. LAS Type E: Dulcimers with Double Bouts, E43. Length: 895 mm .

Marcus and Wade Martin and the Martin Dulcimers (110–12)
Early published works on dulcimers and dulcimer lore consulted by Anne Grimes in her research included those by Charles Faulkner Bryan, Allen H. Eaton, and Charles Seeger. See Selected Bibliography.

In a document, "Selected Slides from Anne Grimes Document Collection: Notes," Grimes wrote that the Moser family—Artus Moser, then a professor at Asheville College, and his daughter, Joan—had instruments made by the Martins that they used for vocal accompaniments in festivals and recordings.

Wade Martin Dulcimer: Sumac, single bout, made by Wade Martin, Swannanoa, North Carolina, early 1950s; Smithsonian Institution Catalog #1996.0276.40.

Marcus Martin Dulcimer: Sumac, cypress and bass wood, single bout, made by Marcus Martin, Swannanoa, North Carolina, 1952; Smithsonian Institution Catalog #1996.0276.38.

Jane Jones McNerlin and the McNerlin Family Dulcimers (113)
In 1974, L. Allen Smith examined both the original Richard Jones dulcimer and the copy of it made by John McNerlin when both dulcimers were in the possession of Roma McNerlin Leonard, in Oak Hill, Ohio. Smith noted the original dulcimer's similarities to Huntington, West Virginia–made dulcimers of the mid-nineteenth century. Information on both instruments is included in LAS under Type E: Dulcimers with Double Bouts. The original is E31, length: 899 mm; the one made by John McNerlin is E35, length: 908 mm.

The National Folk Festival at St. Louis: May Kennedy McCord, Jenny Wells Vincent, Pete Seeger (114–17)
Anne Grimes sang "Ohio River Blues" on her 1957 Folkways Record, *Ohio State Ballads*.

The version of "Ohio River Blues" Anne Grimes sang in St. Louis in 1952 was collected by Mary Wheeler of Paducah, Kentucky, and included in her *Steamboatin' Days, Folk Songs of the River Packet Era* (Baton Rouge: Louisiana State University Press, 1944). Grimes later collected another version of "Ohio River Blues" from Jimmie Lee Pope in Portsmouth, Ohio.

The Voice of America tape-recorded excerpts of the eighteenth annual National Folk Festival in St. Louis in 1952, including Anne Grimes singing "Ohio River Blues," "Canal Dance," "The Nurse Pinched the Baby," and "The Star-Spangled Banner." The recording is in the Archive of Folk Culture at the American Folklife Center, the Library of Congress, LC control #2008700385. Grimes also presented a paper at the 1952 festival, "Ohio History through Folksongs," which is included in her papers.

Sarah Gertrude Knott (1895–1984) organized the first National Folk Festival in St. Louis, Missouri, in 1934.

Anne Grimes referred to May Kennedy McCord as "The Queen of the Ozarks" in her notes: "Nationally known specialist in her native folklore: writer; appeared many times on radio (including her own St. Louis regular program and in Springfield, Mo.) as well as in the movies."

May McCord's version of "Hangman," as collected by Vance Randolph (volume 1), is included in reference to Child ballad #95, "The Maid Freed from the Gallows," in Bertrand Harris Bronson's *The Singing Tradition of Child's Popular Ballads* (Princeton: Princeton University Press, 1976). Booth Campbell also contributed to the Vance Randolph collection (volumes 1, 2, 3, and 4). In her taped interview with Ellen Gibb, Anne Grimes said that her folksong collection most resembles that of Vance Randolph.

Another performer Anne Grimes recorded at the hootenanny was Pleaz Mobley, who recorded for the Library of Congress songs he collected throughout the southeast Kentucky region. He was also a lawyer who at one time served as railroad commissioner for the Third District of Kentucky. (See Ray M. Lawless, *Folksingers and Folksongs in America* [New York: Duell, Sloan, and Pearce, 1960].)

In regard to "Jefferson and Liberty," Anne Grimes wrote the following notes on the song that she performed at a "Heritage of Freedom" school assembly in Newark, Ohio: "Sung in the early 1800's as a campaign song showing the public's delight in doing away with the Alien and Sedition Laws which had delayed immigration and expansion. The music is a wild Irish jig." Date unknown.

After the National Folk Festival in 1953, Anne Grimes and Pete Seeger corresponded and exchanged material. Seeger especially asked about "Ohio River Blues," and he sent to Grimes the lyrics for "Get Off the Track," the abolitionist song with words written in the 1840s by Jesse Hutchinson. Grimes's papers also include correspondence from Booth Campbell, Fred High, May Kennedy McCord, and Carl Sandburg.

Jenny Wells Vincent's rendition of the Mexican folksong "De Los Dorados de Pancho Villa," including the tune and her English translation, appeared in *Sing Out!* 2, no. 12 (June 1952): 12. The song there is nearly the same as the "Pancho Villa" she sang backstage in St. Louis in 1953.

Neva Randolph (118–19)
Anne Grimes sang "My Station's Gonna Be Changed" on her 1957 Folkways record, *Ohio State Ballads*. The lyrics included here are from the Folkways record. The song is one of three she sang on the album that are related to the African American experience in pre–Civil War Ohio. The other two are "My Darling Nelly Gray" and "The Underground Railroad."

The tape of Neva Randolph singing "My Station's Gonna Be Changed" in the Anne Grimes Collection somehow became damaged so that there are skips in the lyrics. Despite this, Neva Randolph's recorded singing of "My Station's Gonna Be Changed" is a favorite of the editors, and is included on the CD.

See Reuben Allen notes above for more information on "The Underground Railroad," and see both Reuben Allen and Bessie Weinrich for other references to "old-style" hymn singing, related to the parody "My Eyes Are Dim."

In her notes on "My Station's Gonna Be Changed," Anne Grimes referenced Mary Ellen Grissom, *The Negro Sings a New Heaven* (Chapel Hill: University of North Carolina Press, 1930); and Howard W. Odum and Guy B. Johnson, *The Negro and His Songs* (Chapel Hill: University of North Carolina Press, 1925).

Eli "Babe" Reno (120–22)
Anne Grimes sang "Portsmouth Fellows" on her 1957 Folkways record *Ohio State Ballads*. Her version was a compilation of texts. Besides the one from Reno, she also collected versions from John Bodiker; Marie Bowers, a Marietta, Ohio, schoolteacher; and Raymond C. Barclay, of Zanesville, in Muskingum County, who taped the song with his children singing along.

Branch Rickey (123–26)
"Branch Rickey's Father" by Edwin Harness Penisten was published by the Ohio Valley Folklore Press, edited by Dave Webb, Folk Publications, New Series, no. 5, a publication of the Ross County Historical Society. Webb, who was among those who worked closely with Anne Grimes in the Ohio Folklore Society, wrote in an editor's preface (under his pseudonym, Erasmus Foster Darby) that Rickey's story about his father rated an important listing in the press's series preserving folk traditions in southern Ohio: "Sports fans in southern Ohio are proud of Branch Rickey and are prone to boast that 'he is a native' and was 'raised up hereabouts' so we must admit he is a folk character already in the region of his birth." A copy of "Branch Rickey's Father" is included in Anne Grimes's contributor file on Branch Rickey.

Branch Rickey's career in public speaking included a series of lectures in the 1920s on the Redpath Chautauqua circuit. In 1926, he was a toastmaster at the annual banquet of the International Lyceum and Chautauqua Association at the Bellevue-Stratford Hotel in Philadelphia.

The "Residue of Design" was part of a set speech Branch Rickey delivered on the lecture circuit that also included a story about Ty Cobb, which he also shared when Anne Grimes tape-recorded him in Upper Arlington, Ohio, in 1954. Rickey said of the Michigan-Minnesota game that he may have erred in some details, but that it was a story that was much talked about and, like the Ty Cobb story, was an actual happening. In fact, although Rickey says that the game took place in Ann Arbor, it actually took place in Minneapolis. His confusion may have been caused in part because in 1926 the

Michigan and Minnesota football teams played against each other twice, the first time in Ann Arbor. Rickey's story refers to the 7–6 win by Michigan in Minneapolis on November 30, 1926. Michigan shared the Big Ten Championship that year with Northwestern. On the Michigan team, in 1926, Benny Friedman was captain and was an All-American with Bennie Oosterbaan. William Flora was All-Conference.

Branch Rickey served as trustee of Ohio Wesleyan University, as did Anne Grimes's mother, Fanny Laylin.

Carl Sandburg (127–28)
Carl Sandburg won the Pulitzer Prize for history in 1940 for his four-volume *Abraham Lincoln: The War Years.* In 1951, he won the Pulitzer Prize for poetry for *Complete Poems by Carl Sandburg.*

Songs from Mary O. Eddy's collection included in Sandburg's *The American Songbag* are "The Quaker's Wooing" and "The Drunkard's Doom." In his later *New American Songbag,* published in 1950, Sandburg included Eddy's "The Lily of the West" and "The Nurse Pinched the Baby."

Abraham Lincoln: The Prairie Years and the War Years, by Carl Sandburg, was published in 1954 by Harcourt, Brace, and Company.

May Kennedy McCord contributed "He Came from His Palace Grand" and "Rolly Trudum" to Sandburg's *New American Songbag.*

Mary Zimmerman was head librarian of the Bexley Public Library for many years and an honorary trustee of the Ohioana Library Association.

Connemara Farm in Flat Rock, North Carolina, is now the Carl Sandburg Home National Historic Site administered by the National Park Service of the U.S. Department of the Interior.

Arthur D. Tyler (129–31)
Anne Grimes sang "Darling Nelly Gray" on her 1957 Folkways record, *Ohio State Ballads.*

The similarity in design noted by Anne Grimes can be seen by comparing the photographs of the Tyler dulcimer made in central Ohio to the dulcimers owned and played traditionally by Bob White, Ken Ward, and Lilly Swick of southeastern Ohio. (See "Dulcerine Players of Southeastern Ohio" in this book.) In a document on Arthur Tyler in the Smithsonian files, Grimes also wrote of the Tyler dulcimer: "Earliest known maker in this tradition seems to have been John Wright, Eno, Gallia County. Round soundholes and mechanical tuners typical of those made after Wright's (1862–1936)."

A photograph of Arthur Tyler was featured on the cover of the August 4, 1957, *Columbus Dispatch Sunday Magazine.* Tyler was one of several Ohio Folklore Society members profiled in an article by Perry Cole entitled "They Keep Folklore Alive," 8–11. Just inside the magazine, an editorial note related to the cover said:

> Historical research has many facets, not least among which is the preservation of songs and stories. Many a clue to the way of life in the past is found in the songs the people sang. The preservation of these too-often forgotten and intangible bits of history is the goal of the Ohio Folklore Society, among whose members is 80-year-old Arthur Tyler of Galloway, whose portrait appears on today's cover, with his homemade dulcimer. Appearing at folklore meetings, however, and recording old-time tunes is by no means Mr. Tyler's chief activity. For instance, when Mac Shaffer came to make the cover photo, Mr. Tyler, while a willing subject, was just a bit impatient to get back to the fields. They were combining wheat that day. But when today's chores are over, Mr. Tyler turns to yesterday, and from the storehouse of his memory he makes a notable contribution toward the preservation of Ohio folklore.

Arthur D. Tyler Dulcimer: Smithsonian Collection Catalogue #1996.0276.23. LAS Type E: Dulcimers with Double Bouts, E46. Length: 912 mm.

William T. Utter and Scheitholts from Licking County (132)
Specializing in midwestern American history and local Licking County lore, William T. Utter was one of several scholars Anne Grimes acknowledged as mentors. Chief among them besides Utter were Claude Simpson, author of the definitive *Music of the British Broadside Ballads,* who taught at Ohio State and later at Stanford; Francis Utley, of the Ohio State University English faculty; and Tristram P. Coffin, who taught English at Denison before becoming head of the folklore department at the University of Pennsylvania. Utter, Simpson, Utley, and Coffin were all active with Grimes in the newly formed Ohio Folklore Society in the early 1950s.

A former mayor of Granville, Ohio, Utter was the author of *Granville, the Story of an Ohio Village,* published in 1956 by the Granville Historical Society. He was chosen by the state of Ohio to write the second volume of a six-volume history of Ohio, *The Frontier State, 1803–1825,* published in 1942.

In a 1952 letter to Anne Grimes, Utter acknowledged the collection of "half a dozen instruments of similar construction" in the Mercer Museum in Doylestown, Pennsylvania, as having helped him identify the scheitholt he contributed to her collection.

Utter/Johnstown Scheitholt: Smithsonian Collection Catalogue #1996.0276.02. LAS Type A: Pennsylvania German Zithers with Straight Sides, A35.

Information about the Tilton family of Granville was published in an article by Minnie Hite Moody, a Granville writer, in her column in the *Newark Advocate,* August 27, 1965.

Tilton Scheitholt: Smithsonian Collection Catalogue #1996.0276.03; LAS Type A: Pennsylvania German Zithers with Straight Sides, A36.

The Aeolian harp donated by Utter to the Anne Grimes Dulcimer Collection was included by Ralph Lee Smith in his 1982 publication, *Three American Folk Instruments,* in which he noted that the instrument's shape of a small slant-top desk suggested that human hands were intended as the playing agent. Anne Grimes in a 1984 letter to a friend said: "Ralph Lee has a point. . . . He neglected to mention that its *eight* (full octave) strings might be further evidence of finger fretting." (Smithsonian Institution Archival Material Related to the Anne Grimes Dulcimer Collection, File 15: Miscellaneous Correspondence.)

Anne Grimes also said in the 1984 letter that Dennis Dorogi—who was then teaching sculpture at Ohio University, Athens, Ohio, and starting to make musical instruments—came to Granville in 1964 to see the Anne Grimes collection for ideas and patterns. In return, he re-glued the Aeolian harp and strung it with G, B, and E guitar strings tuned in unison to low G. Grimes wrote that Dorogi reported his having tested this tuning in a slightly opened window sash with a stiff breeze to find it produced an "ethereal sound."

Aeolian Harp: Smithsonian Collection Catalogue #1996.0276.37.

Another straight-sided, fretted zither in the Anne Grimes Dulcimer Collection is an epinette des Vosges made by Dennis Dorogi in the early 1960s.

Dennis Dorogi Epinette des Vosges: Smithsonian Collection Catalogue #1996.0276.42.

Among other important contributions Utter made to Anne Grimes was the gift to her of a broadside he had found of the ballad "St. Clair's Defeat," which led to her collecting the song from Lottie Leas.

Anne Grimes tape-recorded Bill Utter singing two children's songs, but the tape was accidentally erased. The Grimes contributor file on Utter includes words and notated tunes by Utter for both songs, along with the comment, "My Grandmother Starbuck, b. Clinton Co., 1828, said she learned these tunes at school and that an entire class sang them in unison. I am sure of tunes since we made a game of it when I visited her."

The son of Bill Utter, William L. Utter, in 2009 sent the editors words to a song he remembered his father singing, a song his father told him was a way vowels were learned in school:

> B-a bay-B-E bee,
> B-i Bickibuy
> Bo Bika Buy Bo
> B-u Boo Bicka Bye Bo Boo
> b-i bye.
> B-i-bicka-bye
> Bo bicka bi bo
> B-u Boo Bicka Bye Bo Boo
>
> And on, with
> B-e Bee,
> Etc.

The words remind the editors of some of the "wordplay" recited by Dolleah Church (see above).

Bessie Weinrich (133–40)

In her notes on "The Miller's Will," Anne Grimes suggested for further reference other versions of the song as collected by Sabine Baring-Gould (*Songs of the West: Folk Songs of Devon and Cornwall*); Belden; Brown 2; Cox; Eddy; Flanders, Ballard, Brown, and Barry; Gardner and Chickering; Randolph 1; Sharp 2; and Jean Thomas (*Devil's Ditties*). Grimes also mentioned its inclusion in *Roxburghe Ballads* 8:611, edited by William Chappell (1809–1888). The Roxburghe collection, now held in the British Library, contains over one thousand ballads published in English from 1567 to ca. 1790.

Anne Grimes wrote that all five of her taped contributors of "The Fox" (Carl Gibbs, Mrs. J. W. Haigler, Edna Ross, Edward Starr, and Bessie Weinrich) were from families well-established in Ohio for at least two generations and that their versions were fairly constant, and slightly distant from the one found further out in the Midwest, internationally popularized by Burl Ives.

Anne Grimes owned a rare early printing of sheet music, published in Baltimore in 1837, related to her collected versions of "The Fox." With Grimes's permission, George Perkins of Farleigh Dickinson University made this particular piece of sheet music the subject of an article, "A Pre–Civil War American 'Fox and Goose,'" *Journal of American Folklore* 77, no. 305 (July–September 1964): 263–65.

Anne Grimes collected "My Eyes Are Dim" from several contributors. For more information, see the editors' notes on Reuben Allen.

"The Big Shirt" became a family favorite as well as a favorite of the author, who sang it at her grandson's wedding reception in Ireland. As far as the editors know, this is the first time the song has ever appeared in print, or been heard on CD.

Claude Simpson (1910–1976) taught at Ohio State University from 1947 to 1964. The author of *British Broadside Ballads and Their Music* (1966), among many other scholarly works, he later became Coe Professor of American Literature at Stanford University in California.

Stith Thompson (1885–1976), distinguished service professor of folklore at Indiana University, received international recognition for his six-volume *Motif-Index of Folk-Literature: A Classification of Narrative Elements in Folk Tales, Ballads, Myths, Fables, Mediaeval Romances, Exempla, Fabliaux, Jest-Books, and Local Legends,* first published in 1935, with several revised editions (Indiana University Press). He also served as president of the American Folklore Society, 1937–40.

Faye Wemmer (142–44)

In her notes on "Babes in the Woods," Anne Grimes referenced Brewster; Randolph 1; Sharp 1; and Tolman and Eddy, "Traditional Texts and Tunes," *Journal of American Folklore* 35 (1922): 348. On "There Was a Little Woman," she referenced Opie #535.

Anne Grimes tape-recorded some of the music at the party for the Wemmers in the Grimes home, including "Soldier's Joy," an instrumental with George Wemmer on fiddle and Verna Stupski on piano.

Faye Wemmer's death in 1959 was noted by Ben Hayes in his December 9, 1959, column in the *Columbus Citizen-Journal:* "Mrs. Faye Wemmer, 206 Woodrow Ave., a devoted folklore student, was buried in Athens County last week. At her funeral in Concord Union Church near Jacksonville, Anne Grimes, the folksinger, sang the old hymns."

Bird O. White and Anne White (145–46)

Anne Grimes found references to "Three Jolly Hunters" in Eddy ("Three Jolly Frenchmen"); Flanders, Ballard, Brown, and Barry ("The Three Hunters"); Fuson ("Three Jolly Welshmen"); and Opie #525. She noted that A. B. Graham sang a version of the song he called "The Three Jolly Welshmen," which Grimes said was related to "Beau Reynard" or "Bold Rangers"—a song sung by several other contributors, including Eli "Babe" Reno, who called his version "Portsmouth Fellows."

Anne Rayner Wilson (147–49)

Anne Grimes sang "Logan's Lament" and the related ballad "Battle of Point Pleasant" on her 1957 Folkways record, *Ohio State Ballads.* Her liner notes on both songs include information on historical background, while her bibliography cites under "Ohio and Its History" August C. Mahr's "Indian River and Place Names in Ohio," *Ohio Historical Quarterly* 66 (April 1957), as well as Henry Howe's *Historical Collections of Ohio,* published in various editions from 1847 to 1908, which includes under "Jefferson County" an account of the murder of Logan's family.

August Carl Mahr (1886–1970), who gave Anne Grimes his opinion related to the term "Gehale," was an Ohio State University professor of German and a native speaker of Moravian who in his later years translated the diaries and journals of the Ohio Moravian Missions of Mahikans and Delawares. He also published major studies of comparative Algonkian linguistics, focused on the languages of the Great Lakes. Further information on Mahr is available at the Web sites of both the German and the American Indian Studies departments at Ohio State. The latter Web site also includes a version of "Logan's Lament" under Famous Ohio Speeches.

Mary O. Eddy included "Logan's Lament" or "The Blackbird" in her *Ballads and Songs of Ohio.* She got the J. A. Rayner words and tune from the Ohio Historical Society. The lyrics here are as sung by Anne Grimes on her Folkways record.

Okey Wood and the Okey Wood Dulcimer (150–51)

Anne Grimes's references to "Erin's Green Shore" included Belden, Korson, Laws, Randolph 1, and Thomas (*Devil's Ditties*).

In Anne Grimes's notes on "Naoma Wise," she referred to its collection in Randolph 2 as "Poor Oma Wise," and in *Native American Balladry* by G. Malcolm Laws Jr. as "Poor Omie."

Okey Wood was among eleven contributors to the Anne Grimes Collection who sang "Pearl Bryan" (also titled "The Jealous Lover"). In her notes on the song, Anne Grimes's references to it, and versions of it, include *Native American Balladry* as well as Brewster, Eddy, and Randolph 2.

Okey Wood Dulcimer: Smithsonian Institution Catalogue #1996.0276.26. LAS Type E: Dulcimers with Double Bouts, E63. [Photographs of the Okey Wood dulcimer appear on page 115 of *A Catalogue of Pre-Revival Appalachian Dulcimers.* However, the text on the same page misidentifies the maker and the date the dulcimer was made. Anne Grimes noted this LAS error in a description of E63 that she sent to the

Smithsonian, which correctly identifies the Okey Wood dulcimer in its catalogue.]

Other Contributors of Note

Others of the more than 150 contributors to the Anne Grimes Collection who might be of particular interest to researchers include Eunice Lea Kettering, Lucille Ball Naylor, Howard Barlow, W. M. Kiplinger, and Dr. Raymond C. and Mary Hubbel Osburn.

—Eunice Lea Kettering, the composer, also collected and recorded folksongs in her native Ohio. While on the faculty of Ashland College in Ashland, Ohio, Kettering in 1943 won the National Federation of Music Clubs composition award for her cantata, *Johnny Appleseed.* As music critic of the *Columbus Citizen* at that time, Anne Grimes reported on Kettering's achievement in an article that included this quote from Kettering on folksongs: "If my music shows any trace of their rugged, enduring 'eternal' qualities, I would be most happy indeed. I do not mean outright 'copying' or arranging of folksongs, but a more subtle, intangible something which reminds one of their qualities." Kettering later donated some of her recordings of traditional singers to the Anne Grimes Collection, including Mrs. Adah Drushal of Ashland singing "Come All You Fair and Tender Ladies" (May 30, 1942) and Mrs. Lizzie (G. M.) Knapp of Ashland singing "Twa Sisters," "Lord Thomas and Fair Eleanor," "Barbara Allen," "Drunkard's Song," and "Way Down by the Green Bushes" (May 21, 1941). In 1960, Kettering contributed to Grimes a fine dulcimer that Kettering had bought from the maker, S. F. Russell, at one of the White Top, Virginia, Folk Music Festivals in the 1930s. Kettering wrote in a letter to Grimes that Russell had told her that the wood used in the dulcimer was black walnut, with pegs of maple, and inlay from the keys of an old square piano. "But perhaps he was mistaken," she concluded, "and it is rosewood instead of black walnut. Someday, I shall hope to hear you play it—I always thought I would learn to do a bit with it, but never did take the time, and decided someone like you should have it. And now you *do* have it, and I am so glad, for I really am sentimental about

it—being tied up with memories of White Top—and Mr. Russell himself" (letter dated September 18, 1960, Smithsonian Institution Archival Material Related to the Anne Grimes Dulcimer Collection, File 5: Russell, S. F.). S.F. Russell Dulcimer. Smithsonian Collection Catalogue #1996.0276.10 LAS Type D: Dulcimers with a Single Bout, D15. Length 904 mm.

—Lucille Ball Naylor—a daughter of James Ball Naylor, the author who used midwestern and Indian lore in his successful early-twentieth-century novels—was tape-recorded by Anne Grimes on July 21, 1953, in McConnelsville in Morgan County, Ohio. Among the six songs Naylor sang was "Open the Window, Do Love Do," also known as "Come Love, the Boat Lies Low," that she recalled her father using in his novel, *Ralph Marlow.*

—Howard Barlow, the orchestral, radio, and television conductor, was tape-recorded by Anne Grimes on October 24, 1953, singing a fragment of "The Cuckoo." He learned the song from his Grandfather Barlow, who was born in Ohio and whose father served on Gen. George Washington's staff in the Revolutionary War.

—W. M. Kiplinger, journalist and founder of the *Kiplinger Newsletter.* Born near Bellefontaine, Ohio, in Logan County in 1891, Kiplinger was one of the first two journalism graduates from Ohio State University in 1912. Anne Grimes met Kiplinger when he was in Columbus in 1956 to receive an award from the Ohioana Library. He subsequently sent to Grimes a ballad he tape-recorded in Washington, D.C., entitled "The Days of Forty-Nine."

—Dr. Raymond C. Osburn. Holder of many offices of distinction in scientific societies, Dr. Osburn was emeritus chairman of the sociology and entomology department of Ohio State University when Anne Grimes on November 23, 1953, tape-recorded him and his wife, Mary Hubbel Osburn, who was a singer, composer, and author of *Ohio Composers and Musical Authors.* Dr. Osburn talked about learning songs from his father in Licking County, Ohio. The Osburns sang seven songs, including "Peter Gray," "Go Tell Aunt Rhodie," and "Boston Burglar."

Author's Acknowledgments

Collectors/Scholars: Early Help, Sponsors, and Inspiration

Tristram P. Coffin: Internationally eminent folklore and ballad scholar. Initially active with Anne Grimes in the Ohio Folklore Society when he was a professor at Denison University. Among those scholars who introduced Grimes to folklore scholarship and contacts, helping her identify and classify significant collectanea and suggesting subsequent papers and articles. Active with Grimes in the newly founded Ohio Folklore Society. Later joined the faculty of the University of Pennsylvania. His publications include *The British Traditional Ballad in North America.* Secretary/Treasurer of the American Folklore Society (1961–65).

Mary O. Eddy: Perrysville, Ohio, folk music and hymnology authority; collector and published scholar. Active with Grimes in Federation of Music Clubs folk music projects and a valuable contact with informants and authorities, including Carl Sandburg and George Pullen Jackson. Her *Ballads and Songs from Ohio* (published 1939, reprinted 1964 with a foreword by D. K. Wilgus) considered by Grimes to be definitive for the state. Longtime Grimes friend, teacher, and sponsor.

Royal D. Hughes: Founder and chair of the Ohio State University Department (now School) of Music. Grimes's music history professor and graduate advisor.

Elizabeth Yarrow Mansfield: OSU faculty wife who as a Vassar graduate student had done field recordings for Elizabeth Greenleaf's *Ballads and Songs of Newfoundland* (Harvard University Press, l933). Also a fine musician who widened the scope of Grimes's collection and research techniques.

Ruth Ann Musick: Folk music and folktale authority, especially of West Virginia. Scholar, collector, editor, publisher. PhD professor of mathematics at Fairmont State College. One of the first to recognize the potential significance of Grimes's work as a performer/collector, as well as the importance of Grimes's early "finds." Contributed to Grimes's research expertise and provided productive informant and scholar contacts, including Vance Randolph and John Jacob Niles.

Harry Ridenour: Collector/performer, ballad and Shakespeare authority, professor at Baldwin-Wallace College in Berea, Ohio, where he inspired many career students. Many years' association with Grimes in state and local folklore societies, for which they frequently did co-performances. Generously recommended her lecture-recitals, aided her research, and gave her informant "leads."

Claude Simpson: A special inspiration as a scholar/musician (an accomplished fellow pianist). Active with Grimes in the Ohio Folklore Society. Continued to help and advise her after he left Ohio State University for the faculty of Stanford University. Author of the definitive *Music of the British Broadside Ballads*.

Cloea Thomas: Ohio State University music education faculty; also Grimes's elementary school music teacher. With Edith Keller (see below) recorded/researched the important Captain Pearl R. Nye canal folksong material. Used Grimes as singer for presentations and research of Nye material.

Francis Utley: Ohio State University English faculty and first president of the Ohio Folklore Society, founded in 1950. Prominent medievalist. Initially furthered Grimes's confidence and recognition by using a recording of her singing to illustrate his American Folklore Society Meeting paper on "The Foggy Dew." President of the American Folklore Society (1951–52).

William L. Utter: Professor and chair of the Denison University history department. Furthered Grimes's enthusiasm for and knowledge of Midwest and Ohio history. Contributed to the start of her collection of dulcimers and traditional plucked instruments. Reviewed her Folkways record for the *Ohioana Quarterly,* the journal of the Ohioana Library.

Major Ohio: All Longtime Friends, Teachers, and Supporters

Elizabeth Wilson Ahler: Denison University music faculty and national concert artist; Grimes's singing teacher.

A. B. Graham: 4-H Clubs founder; shared with Grimes his interest and knowledge of midwestern lore and supplied numerous contacts.

Ben Hayes: *Columbus Citizen* columnist. Former colleague of Grimes on the newspaper, supplied contacts and wrote about Grimes and her contributors.

Burris Hiatt: History professor, Wilmington College, Ohio; expert in Quaker, abolitionist, and Underground Railroad lore.

Edith Keller: State director in Ohio of music education and a family friend. Shared her knowledge of the traditional music of every county in the state with Grimes; set up and often went with her to numerous and varied performance occasions; provided informant leads and was continually supportive in Grimes's long-range collection aims.

Eunice Kettering: Ashland College faculty; eminent composer using folk music themes. Donated material from her taped collection of traditional Ohio singers to the Anne Grimes taped collection. Also donated a fine dulcimer to the Anne Grimes dulcimer collection.

Grace Hamilton Morrey: Performing artist-pianist; Grimes's piano and music theory teacher; head of Morrey School of Music in which Grimes studied from age five through high school.

Carolyn Piercy: Cleveland, Ohio, authority and author on Shaker lore.

Rebecca Schroeder: University of Missouri; corresponded on Ohio and canal folksong research.

Marie Hertenstein Waller: Performing artist-pianist. Grimes's piano teacher.

David Webb: Chillicothe, Ohio, folklore collector and publisher. Involved in work with Grimes in the Ohio Folklore Society. A Grimes "fan" who also set up research, informant "leads," and lecture-recital dates for her.

Mary Wheeler: Kentucky collector/author. Ohio River folksongs.

Dulcimer: Exchange and Encouragement

Charles F. Bryan: Tennessee music professor. Pioneer dulcimer collector, researcher, and performer. Exchanged information with Grimes and arranged her appearances to deliver papers and programs for folklore societies and schools.

John Jacob Niles: Collector, composer, ballad singer, dulcimer authority. Longtime Grimes acquaintance/mentor.

John Putnam: Dulcimer expert and writer; Berea College and Washington, D.C.

Howie Mitchell: Dulcimer maker and player (and physicist) in Washington, D.C.

Jean Ritchie and Edna Ritchie Baker: Corresponded with Jean; met and exchanged material with Edna.

Internationally Recognized Folklorists and Performers

Annabel Morris Buchanan: Tennessee composer, collector, author, and officer of the National Federation of Music Clubs, for which Grimes served as the regional folk music archivist for the Central Eastern Region (Indiana, Ohio, Pennsylvania, New Jersey, Delaware, Maryland, Washington, D.C., and West Virginia).

Helen Hartness Flanders: New England authority; collector/author whose published collections served as Grimes's models. Visited Grimes and compared research techniques and collections' similarities.

Edith Fowke: Canadian and British ballad collector/author.

Kenneth S. Goldstein: International folklore authority. Recorder/editor of Grimes's Folkways record. President of the American Folklore Society (1975–76).

Archie Green: Labor songs. Lobbied (with Grimes's help) for the creation of the American Folklife Center, established by Congress in 1976.

John Greenway: Labor and protest folksongs and ballads. Editor of the *Journal of American Folklore* (1964–68).

Joseph Hickerson: Director of the Archive of Folk Song/Culture at the Library of Congress (1974–98). Acknowledged Grimes's influence in his decision to pursue a folk music career after meeting her when he was a senior at Oberlin College (physics major). Facilitated the transfer of Grimes's collection tapes and related materials to the Library of Congress in 1995.

Frank Hoffman: Authority on bawdy and other folksongs; published booklet on West Virginia ballads for which Grimes wrote the introduction.

Rae Korson: Head, Archive of Folk Song at the Library of Congress (1955–69); facilitated the reproduction of Grimes's collection tapes for the Library of Congress in 1958.

Bascom Lamar Lunsford: North Carolina folk music/ballad authority/performer. Founded Mountain Dance and Folk Festival in Asheville, at which Grimes performed. An Ohio Folklore Society speaker.

Carl Sandburg: Grimes mentor.

Pete Seeger: Participated with Grimes in National Folk Festival. Helped research and establish significance of (exchanged) material.

Ellen Stekert and J. Barre Toelken: Both eminent scholars and performers and longtime Grimes associates. Presidents of the American Folklore Society in successive years: Stekert in 1977, Toelken in 1978.

D. K. Wilgus: Active in the Ohio Folklore Society with Grimes when he was a student at Ohio State University; later, while teaching at Western Kentucky State College, served with Grimes as co-regional archivist (Southeastern Region) in the National Federation of Music Clubs. Author of *Anglo-American Folksong Scholarship since 1898.* President of the American Folklore Society (1971–72).

Additional Acquaintances, Mainly through Grimes's Activity in or Performance at State and National Historical and Folklore Societies and Festivals

George C. Grise: English professor at Austin Peay State College in Clarksville, Tennessee; collector/singer, participant with Grimes in National Festivals; sponsor for her Kentucky and Tennessee folklore society papers and university programs.

Wayland Hand: President of the American Folklore Society (1957–58).

William Hugh Jansen: Professor of English, folklorist, University of Kentucky.

Sarah Gertrude Knott: Founder and director of the National Folk Festival in which Grimes was a participant and board member.

MacEdward Leach: Ballad authority. President of the American Folklore Society (1961–62).

Beatrice Kane McClain: University of Alabama; authority on Southern folk music.

W. Edson Richmond: Professor of English and folklore at Indiana University.

Ruth Rubin: Folksinger, ethnomusicologist, collector. Author of *A Treasury of Jewish Folk Song.* Her records include *Jewish Folksongs* and *Jewish Life* on Folkways.

Editors' Acknowledgments

THANK YOU TO ALL who gave us permission to quote their words and to include their singing and playing or that of their parents, grandparents, great-grandparents, aunts, uncles, and other relations. We tried to contact everyone featured in the book, or their descendants, and in most cases we were successful. However, some we could not find. If anyone reading this knows of someone who is a direct descendant of any of the singers or players presented in this book, we would be most pleased to hear from them.

We want to thank the following people, and especially those who took time to share valuable information—whether in phone conversations, letters, or e-mails:

Kelly Urban, great-grandson of Frank and Miriam Allen

Gertrude Green, daughter of Reuben Allen

Neill Pauff, grandson of John M. Bodiker

Norma Luellen, granddaughter of
Sarah Basham and niece of Bertha Basham Wright

Todd Bogatay, son of Paul and Hennie Bogatay

Gary White, son of Bob White; and Gary's wife, Sharon

Kendra Ward, daughter of Ken Ward

Meridian Green and Susan G. Hartnett,
daughters of Bob Gibson; and to the bobgibsonlegacy.com Web site

Walter Dixon III, grandson of Walter Dixon

Phyllis Townsend, granddaughter of Blanche Fullen

Marilyn Hurless, granddaughter of A. B. Graham

Michael D. Halley, grandson of Brodie Franklin Halley

Ronald H. Harper, grandson of Perry Harper

Wanda Ball, granddaughter of Amanda Styers Hook

Edna T. Lunsford, widow of Lamar Lunsford,
son of Bascom Lamar Lunsford

Frances S. Martin, widow of Wade Martin

Henry Janss, grandson of May Kennedy McCord

Pete Seeger

Jenny Wells Vincent

Forest J. Farmer Sr., grandson of Neva Randolph; and Forest J. Farmer Jr., her great-grandson

Ottie Reno, son of Babe and Arbannah Reno

Branch Rickey III, grandson of Branch Rickey

The Carl Sandburg Family Trust and its attorney, Susan Taylor Rash

William L. Utter, son of William T. Utter

Philip Weinrich, grandson of Bessie Weinrich

Verna P. Stupski, daughter of Faye Wemmer

Mary Ann Ross, daughter of Okey Wood; and sons Glen R. Wood and French D. Wood; daughter, Orma McLaughlin; and daughter-in-law, Beatrice Wood

Thank you to Judith Gray, Jennifer Cutting, and Todd Harvey at the American Folklife Center of the Library of Congress; to Stacey Kluck, Jane Rogers, and Jane Woodall at the Smithsonian Institution; and to Margot Nassau, Stephanie Smith, and Jeff Place at Smithsonian Folkways Recordings.

Thank you to Ohio University Press, most especially to our editors Nancy Basmajian and Gillian Berchowitz, and to our book designer, Julie Elman, assistant professor in the School of Visual Communication at Ohio University in Athens.

Thank you to early readers of the book for their advice and encouragement: David Kay, Marsha Marotta, Arlene Matzkin, Lawrence Pinkham, and Carlotta and Ran Shaw.

Thank you to all the research librarians, archivists, and others who assisted, including Lisa Wood, audiovisual curator, and Elizabeth L. Plummer, assistant department head, research services archives/library collections at the Ohio Historical Society; Mary Frechette, Fine Arts Dept., St. Louis Public Library; Jeanelle Ash, curator at the Ralph Foster Museum at the College of the Ozarks; and Jennifer Ford, head of archives and special collections and associate professor at the University of Mississippi.

Thank you to those who responded so positively to requests for help: Joe Hickerson, Barbara Vogel, Robert Force, Rochelle Goldstein, Diane Pacetti of the *Lima News;* Constance Reik, Andy Murphy of the *Columbus Dispatch;* Terry S. Morgan, L. Allen Smith, Scott Dorsey, and Marji Hazen and the Hazen Folk Music Collection at the Ashland University (Ohio) Archives.

We are grateful to Smithsonian Folkways Recordings for permission to reprint excerpts from the liner notes accompanying *Ohio State Ballads,* Folkways 05217, © 1957. A download of these liner notes is available at the Smithsonian Folkways Web site at no cost.

We are grateful to everyone who helped produce our CD, including Tess Rock and Samantha Rock for listening to early CD drafts; Judith Gray and the American Folklife Center of the Library of Congress for transferring from tape to CD Anne Grimes's singing of "John Funston," which is part of their holdings; Lisa Wood at the Ohio Historical Society for facilitating the physical transfer of tapes held in the Anne Grimes Collection there for processing at the Musicol Recording Studio in Columbus, Ohio; John Hull and Warren Hull at Musicol for their engineering the transfer of our selections from the OHS tapes to CD; and Bruce Gigax and Reed Wheeler at Audio Recording Studio in Bentleyville, Ohio, for assembling and editing our master CD.

Thank you to Judith McCulloh for her wise counsel.

On a personal note, we all have many people to thank who have sustained and encouraged us, but none more so than Ronnie Graham, David Kay, Sean Kay, Anna Marie Madigan Kay, Cria Anne Kay, Siobhan Mattie Kay, and Alana Rose Kay.

Finally, a special thanks to our brother, Steve Grimes, without whom this book would not have been possible.

Selected Bibliography

Anne Grimes conducted much of her research in her own library of music books. Most of the following were in her library, some inscribed personally to her by the authors, including Mary O. Eddy, Helen Hartness Flanders, Caroline B. Piercy, Carl Sandburg, L. Allen Smith, Ralph Lee Smith, and Mary Wheeler.

Books

Andrews, Edward D. *The Gift to Be Simple: Songs, Dances and Rituals of the American Shakers.* New York: J. J. Augustin, 1940.

Bareis, Geo. F. *History of Madison Township, Including Groveport and Canal Winchester, Franklin County, Ohio.* Canal Winchester, OH: Geo. F. Bareis, 1902.

Beattie, John W. *The American Singer.* Book 6. New York: American Book Company, 1951.

Belden, H. M. *Ballads and Songs, Collected by the Missouri Folk-Lore Society.* University of Missouri Studies 15, no. 1. Columbia: University of Missouri, 1955.

Brewster, Paul G., ed. *Ballads and Songs of Indiana.* Indiana University Publications, Folklore Series. Bloomington: Indiana University, 1940.

Brink, Carol. *Harps in the Wind: The Story of the Singing Hutchinsons.* New York: Macmillan, 1947.

Bronson, Bertrand Harris. *The Traditional Tunes of the Child Ballads.* 4 vols. Princeton, NJ: Princeton University Press, 1959–72.

———, ed. *The Singing Tradition of Child's Popular Ballads.* Princeton, NJ: Princeton University Press, 1976.

Brown, Frank C. *The Frank C. Brown Collection of North Carolina Folklore.* Vol. 2, *Folk Ballads from North Carolina.* Edited by Henry M. Belden and Arthur Palmer Hudson. Durham, NC: Duke University Press, 1952.

———. *The Frank C. Brown Collection of North Carolina Folklore.* Vol. 3, *Folk Songs from North Carolina.* Edited by Henry M. Belden and Arthur Palmer Hudson. Durham, NC: Duke University Press, 1952.

Buckley, Bruce R. *Ballads and Folksongs in Scioto County, Ohio.* MA thesis, Ohio Folklore Archives, Miami (Ohio) University, 1952.

Child, Francis J. *The English and Scottish Popular Ballads, 1882–98.* Reproduction of 1883–98 ed. New York: Folklore Press, 1956.

Cox, John Harrington. *Folk-Songs of the South, Collected under the Auspices of the West Virginia Folk-Lore Society.* Reprint of 1925 Harvard University Press edition. New York: Dover, 1967.

Cray, Ed, ed. *The Erotic Muse, A Completely Uncensored Collection of the Songs Everybody Knows and No One Has Written Down Before.* New York: Oak, 1969. Second edition as *The Erotic Muse: American Bawdy Songs.* Urbana: University of Illinois Press, 1992.

Davis, Arthur Kyle, Jr., ed. *Traditional Ballads of Virginia, Collected under the Auspices of the Virginia Folk-Lore Society.* Cambridge, MA: Harvard University Press, 1929.

Eaton, Allen H. *Handicrafts of the Southern Highlands.* Containing Fifty-eight Illustrations from Photographs Taken for the Work by Doris Ulmann. New York: Russell Sage Foundation, 1937.

Eddy, Mary O., ed. *Ballads and Songs from Ohio.* New York: J. J. Augustin, 1939.

Finger, Charles. *Frontier Ballads.* Garden City, NY: Doubleday Page, 1927.

Flanders, Helen Hartness, Elizabeth Flanders Ballard, George Brown, and Phillips Barry, eds. *The New Green Mountain Songster: Traditional Folk Songs of Vermont.* New Haven, CT: Yale University Press, 1939.

Flanders, Helen Hartness, and Marguerite Olney. *Ballads Migrant in New England.* Introduction by Robert Frost. New York: Farrar, Straus and Young, 1953.

Force, Robert, and Albert d'Ossche. *In Search of the Wild Dulcimer.* New York: Vintage Books, 1974.

Fuson, Henry Harvey. *Ballads of the Kentucky Highlands.* London: Mitre, 1931.

Gardner, Emelyn Elizabeth, and Geraldine Jencks Chickering, eds. *Ballads and Songs of Southern Michigan.* Ann Arbor: University of Michigan Press, 1939.

Greenleaf, Elisabeth Bristol, ed. *Ballads and Sea Songs of Newfoundland.* Music recorded in the field by Grace Yarrow Mansfield and the editor. Cambridge, MA: Harvard University Press, 1933.

High, Fred. *It Happened in the Ozarks.* Berryville, AR: n.p., 1954.

Howe, Henry. *Historical Collections of Ohio.* Cincinnati: C. J. Krehbiel, various editions from 1847 to 1908.

Hudson, Arthur Palmer. *Folksongs of Mississippi and Their Background.* Chapel Hill: University of North Carolina Press, 1936.

Jackson, George Pullen, ed. *Down-East Spirituals and Others: Three Hundred Songs Supplementary to the Author's Spiritual Folk-Songs of Early America.* 2nd ed. Locust Valley, NY: J. J. Augustin, 1953.

Korson, George, ed. *Coal Dust on the Fiddle: Songs and Stories of the Bituminous Industry.* Philadelphia: University of Pennsylvania Press, 1943.

——. *Pennsylvania Songs and Legends.* Philadelphia: University of Pennsylvania Press, 1949.

Lawless, Ray M. *Folksingers and Folksongs in America, A Handbook of Biography, Bibliography, and Discography.* New York: Duell, Sloan and Pearce, 1960. Anne Grimes's biography is on pages 100–102: "All this—the children, the collecting and singing, the study and writing—adds up to a busy and fascinating career for one of America's important contemporary folksingers." Includes photo of Grimes and her dulcimer collection.

Laws, G. Malcolm, Jr. *American Balladry from British Broadsides: A Guide for Students and Collectors of Traditional Song.* Publications of the American Folklore Society, Bibliographical and Special Series 8. Philadelphia: American Folklore Society, 1957.

Laylin, Clarence D. *Norwalk in the Nineties.* Columbus: Ohio Historical Society, 1970.

Lomax, John A., and Alan Lomax, eds. *American Ballads and Folk Songs.* Foreword by George Lyman Kittredge. New York: Macmillan, 1946.

———, eds. *Our Singing Country: A Second Volume of American Ballads and Folk Songs.* Ruth Crawford Seeger, music editor. New York: Macmillan, 1949.

Morris, Alton C., ed. *Folksongs of Florida.* Musical transcriptions by Leonhard Deutsch. Gainesville: University of Florida Press, 1950.

Nye, Pearl R., and Cloea Thomas. *Scenes and Songs of the Ohio-Erie Canal.* Columbus: Ohio Historical Society, 1971.

Opie, Iona, and Peter Opie, eds. *The Oxford Dictionary of Nursery Rhymes.* Oxford: Clarendon Press, 1951.

Piercy, Caroline B. *The Shaker Cook Book: Not by Bread Alone.* Illustrated by Virginia Filson Walsh. General editor, Virginia Filson Walsh. New York: Crown, 1953.

———. *The Valley of God's Pleasure: A Saga of the North Union Shaker Community.* New York: Stratford House, 1951.

Randolph, Vance, ed. *Ozark Folksongs.* 4 vols. Columbia: State Historical Society of Missouri, 1946–50.

———. *Pissing in the Snow and Other Ozark Folktales.* Urbana: University of Illinois Press, 1976.

Sandburg, Carl, comp. *The American Songbag.* New York: Harcourt, Brace, 1927.

———, comp. *Carl Sandburg's New American Songbag.* New York: Broadcast Music, 1950.

Sargent, Helen Child, and George Lyman Kittredge, eds. *English and Scottish Popular Ballads, Edited from the Collection of Francis James Child.* Boston: Houghton Mifflin, 1904.

Sharp, Cecil J., comp. *English Folksongs from the Southern Appalachians.* Edited by Maud Karpeles and Geoffrey Cumberlege. 2 vols. London: Oxford University Press, 1932.

Simpson, Claude M. *The British Broadside Ballad and Its Music.* New Brunswick, NJ: Rutgers University Press, 1966.

Smith, L. Allen. *A Catalogue of Pre-Revival Appalachian Dulcimers.* Foreword by Jean Ritchie. Columbia: University of Missouri Press, 1983. In a footnote to his preface, Smith acknowledged Anne Grimes as an authority on the dulcimer: "Anne Grimes is responsible for much fieldwork in Ohio and has influenced the work of many folklorists since the 1950s." His book includes twenty-eight instruments from the Anne Grimes Dulcimer Collection, with photographs, pages 25, 31, 33, 40, 43, 50, 51, 52, 59, 62, 64, 67, 68, 75, 80, 100, 102, 103, 104, 105, 106, 111, 115, and 116.

Smith, Ralph Lee. *The Story of the Dulcimer.* Cosby, TN: Crying Creek, 1986. In an appendix on preservers of dulcimers, Smith wrote: "The first really substantial collection of old dulcimers, as opposed to scheitholts, was assembled in the years following World War II by Anne Grimes, a folksinger and folklorist of Granville, Ohio. . . . This important collection not only illuminates the history of the dulcimer in the mountains, but includes instruments, found in Ohio, which clearly document the traditional presence of both dulcimers and scheitholts north and west of the Ohio River."

——. *Three American Folk Instruments: Box Zithers, Scheitholts, Dulcimers.* Reston, VA: Press at Chimney House Road, 1982.

Smith, Reed. *South Carolina Ballads, with a Study of the Traditional Ballad To-day.* Cambridge, MA: Harvard University Press, 1928.

Thomas, Jean. *Devil's Ditties, Being Stories of the Kentucky Mountain People.* Chicago: W. Wilbur Hatfield, 1931.

Thomas, Jean, and Joseph A. Leeder. *The Singin' Gatherin': Tunes from the Southern Appalachians.* New York: Silver, Burdett, 1939.

Wheeler, Mary. *Steamboatin' Days: Folk Songs of the River Packet Era.* Baton Rouge: Louisiana State University Press, 1944.

Wilson, Frazer E. *Arthur St. Clair, Rugged Ruler of the Old Northwest: An Epic of the American Frontier.* Richmond, VA: Garrett and Massie, 1944.

WPA. *The Ohio Guide.* Compiled by workers of the Writers' Program of the Work Projects Administration in the State of Ohio. sponsored by the Ohio State Archaeological and Historical Society. American Guide Series. New York: Oxford University Press, 1940; 7th printing 1956.

Articles

Blomstedt, Erik. "Anne Grimes Dulcimer Research Pioneer." *Dulcimer Players News* 2, no. 1 (Winter 1985): 4–7. With photos.

Bryan, Charles Faulkner. "American Folk Instruments: I. The Appalachian Mountain Dulcimer." *Tennessee Folklore Society Bulletin* 18, no. 1 (March 1952): 1–5.

——. "The Appalachian Mountain Dulcimer Enigma." *Tennessee Folklore Society Bulletin* 20, no. 4 (December 1954): 86–90.

Grimes, Anne. Article-review of *The Shaker Cook Book: Not by Bread Alone* by Caroline Piercy. *Ohio Archaeological and Historical Quarterly* 63 (January 1954): 83–85.

——. "Dulcerine Feature of Museum Exhibit." *Columbus Dispatch,* March 27, 1955, 12E.

——. "The Dulcimer, Only American Folk-Designed Musical Instrument." *Ohioana Library Engagement Calendar Year Book,* Vol. 20—Early Ohio, 1967, page 48.

——. "Ohio in Song." *Ohio Music Club News* 10, no. 3 (Spring 1952): 10.

——. *Ohio State Ballads.* Edited by Kenneth S. Goldstein. Folkways Records. Sixteen-page brochure on songs in the record album, with bibliography, 1957. Included with cassette and CD reissues by Smithsonian/Folkways.

——. Review of *Richard the Shaker. Journal of the Ohio Folklore Society,* new series, 2, no. 3 (Winter 1973): 29–37. Also an abstract of a talk delivered by Anne Grimes, "Bodiker's Bawdy Ballads," at the Spring 1973 Ohio Folklore Society Meeting, pp. 46–47.

——. Review of *Dan Emmett and the Rise of Early Negro Minstrelsy,* by Hans Nathan. *Ohioana: Of Ohio and Ohioans* 6 (Winter 1963): 99–102.

Hoffman, Frank A. *Some West Virginia Songs and Ballads,* with introduction by Anne Grimes, Ohio Valley Folk Research Project. Chillicothe, Ohio: Ross County Historical Society, 1959.

Legman, Gershon. "The Bawdy Song . . . in Fact and in Print." *Explorations: Studies in Culture and Communication* 7 (March 1957): 139–56. Expanded as a chapter in *The Horn Book: Studies in Erotic Folklore and Bibliography* (New Hyde Park, NY: University Books, 1964), 336–426.

——. "'Unprintable' Folklore? The Vance Randolph Collection." *Journal of American Folklore* 103, no. 409 (July–September 1990): 259–300.

Midwest Folklore 3, no. 1 (Spring 1953). Published by Indiana University, Bloomington, with Ohio folklore articles by Bruce R. Buckley, Tristram P. Coffin, Mary O. Eddy, Anne Grimes and others. Grimes's article starts on page 47: "Possible Relationship Between 'Jump Jim Crow' and Shaker Songs."

Olsen, J. P. "The Ballad of Anne Grimes." *Ohio Magazine,* January 1994, 38–40 and 71–72.

Seeger, Charles. "The Appalachian Dulcimer." *Journal of American Folklore* 71, no. 279 (January–March 1958): 40–51.

Smith, L. Allen. "Toward a Reconstruction of the Development of the Appalachian Dulcimer: What the Instruments Suggest." *Journal of American Folklore* 93, no. 370 (October–December 1980): 385–86.

Tolman, Albert H. and Eddy, Mary O. "Traditional Texts and Tunes." *Journal of American Folklore* 35, no. 138 (October–December 1922): 335–442.

Sheet Music

"The Fox and the Goose." Baltimore, 1837. Probable earliest American sheet music printing of this medieval carol survival. See Editors' Notes on Bessie Weinrich.

Subject Index

A page number in italic type indicates an illustration.

The letter *n* following a page number indicates an Editors' Note.

dulcimers (dulcerines) *(continued)*
John McNerlin dulcimer, *112*; McNerlin heirloom dulcimer, 112; Marcus Martin dulcimer, 110, 111; Middletown dulcimer, *vi, 9*, 10; Okey Wood dulcimer, *150, 152*; scantling, *18,* 19; Singleton dulcimer, 20; Tilton scheitholt, *132;* Tyler dulcimer, *129;* Wade Martin dulcimer, 8, *110,* 111, *116. See also* Butcher, George; Chacey, Ron; McNerlin, John; Wright, John

Eddy, Mary O., 72, 88, 127
Emmett, Dan, 3, 10, 31

Fenstermaker, Ella, 89
Fields, Arthur Byrd, 63–64, 158–59n
Fields, Bill, 63
Flack, Ella Strawser, 65–67, *68,* 142, 159n
Flora, William, 125
Folksmiths, The, ix
Folkways Records, ix, 1–2, 3
Frost, Elizabeth, 56
Fullen, Blanche Wilson, 68–71, 159n

Gibb, Ellen, 7, 16
Gibson, Bob, ix, 14, 72–74, 159–60n
Gibson, Rose, 72, 73
Graham, A. B., xi, 75–76, 160n
Granville, Ohio, 15, 33, 36, 132
Grimes, Anne, ix, xi; ca. 1957, *11;* with her children, *1, 5;* at home, 1987, *13;* at home, early 1960s, *8;* at home, mid-1980s, *17;* Margaret O. Moody and, 1955, *7;* Middletown dulcimer and, *vi,* 8, *9;* Mrs. Frances Kelley and, 1953, *6;* Mrs. J. W. Haigler and, 1955, *4;* performing at the National Folk Festival, St Louis, 1952–53, *114, 116;* performing in Dayton, 1953, *54;* Wade Martin dulcimer and, *110*
Grimes, James W. "Jimmie," ix, *5,* 6, 19, 53, 58, 113; Asheville, NC, and, 106; at Denison University, 132; Ohio Historical Society and, 6, 132; at Ohio State University, 6
Grimes, Steve, *xi, 1, 5*
Growden, Bessie, *68*

Hagerman, Adeline Palmer Hughes, *96,* 97
Hagerman, Edward, 97
Haigler, Mrs. J. W., 4
Halley, Brodie Franklin, 77–79, 160n
Hanby, Benjamin Russell, 3, 131
Harding, Warren G., 54–55
Harper, Perry, 80–83, 160n
Hayes, Ben, 11, 42: on Dolly Church, 52–53
Hayes, Rutherford B., 75
Heckendorn, Harold, 16
Hickerson, Joe, x, 16
High, Fred: *It Happened in the Ozarks,* 115
Hill Town Folk Festival, 12
Hook, Amanda Styers, 84–86, 142, 145, 160n

Keller, Edith, 136
Kendal at Oberlin, x, 16
Kieffer, Arthur Emerson, 87–90, 160n
Kipke, Harry, 124–26
Knott, Sarah Gertrude, 114
Korson, Rae (Mrs. George), ix

Langstaff, Donald, 91–94, 160–61n

Laylin Clarence D., 3
Laylin, Fanny Hagerman, 3, 95–101, 158n, 161–62n
Laylin, Lewis Cass, 55
Leas, Lottie, 102–5, 162–63n
Legman, Gershon, 49
Library of Congress, 15
lining out, 22, 63, 118, 135
Logan's Elm, 148
Lunsford, Bascom Lamar, 14, 42, 106–7, 163n
Lunsford, W. E. "Eddie," 108–9, 163n; John H. Lunsford dulcimer
    and, 108–9

Magnecorder, 4, *34*
Mahr, August C., 148
Martin, Marcus, 8, 106, 110–11, 163n
Martin, Wade, 8, 106, 110–11, 163n
McCord, May Kennedy, 114–15, 127–28, 163–64n
McJunkin, Penelope Niven, 16
McNerlin, Jane Jones, and the McNerlin family dulcimers, 98,
    112–13, 163n
McNerlin, John, 113
Moody, Margaret O., 7, 32, 156n
Morgan, Ruth S., 12
Morrison, Frank, 91
Mountain Dance and Folk Festival, 8, 106–7, 111. *See also* Lunsford,
    Bascom Lamar

National Federation of Music Clubs, ix
National Folk Festival, 1; Nashville, 1959, 42; St. Louis, 1952, 114; St.
    Louis, 1953, 114–17, 163–64n. *See also* McCord, May Kennedy;
    Seeger, Pete; Vincent, Jenny Wells
New American Songbag (Sandburg), 114
Newton, Vic, 121
Niles, John Jacob, 111
Nye, Captain Pearl R., 31

O'Brien, "Wyoming Jack," *116*
Ohio Arts Council, 16
Ohio counties, map of, *2*
Ohio Folklore Society, ix, xii, 7, 8, 15, 68; Henry Lawrence Beecher and,
    35; John Bodiker and, 42; Dolleah Church and, 51; Bob Gibson
    and, 72; A. B. Graham and, 76; Anne Grimes, president, ix, 7;
    Bascam Lamar Lunsford and, 106; W. E. Lunsford and, 109;
    Arthur Tyler and, 130; Faye Wemmer and, 142
Ohio Hills Folk Festival poster, *12*
Ohio Historical Society, xii, 6, 15, 16, 132
Ohio State Ballads (Folkways), 10
Ohio State University, xii, 3, 6; Distinguished Career in Music Award, 15
Ohio Valley Folklore Press, 123
Ohio Wesleyan University, xii, 3; Alumni Association's Distinguished
    Achievement Citation, 15
Oosterbaan, Bennie, 124–25

Patterson, Jefferson, 54
Piercy, Carolyn, 56–57

Quaker City Home Towner, 12–14

Ralston, Charles, *61,* 62, 158n
Randolph, Neva, 118–19, 164n
Randolph, Vance: *Ozark Folksongs,* 114
Rayner, J. A., 148

Reno, Arbannah, 120
Reno, Eli "Babe," 120–22, 164n
Rickey, Branch, 123–26, 164–65n
Ritchie, Jean, 19

Sandburg, Carl, 8, 127–28, 165n
Sander's Fourth Reader, 147
scantling, *18,* 19
scheitholts, 132
Schlupp, Frank, 89
Seeger, Pete, ix, 15, 73, 115, 164n
Shakers, 56–57
Sheppard, Jason, 78
Sidle, David V., 91
Sidle, Kenny, 91
Simpson, Claude, 136
Simpson, Joshua McCarty, 22
Singin' Gatherin', The (Thomas), 111
Singleton, Will, 19–20
Smith, L. Allen: *A Catalogue of Pre-Revival Appalachian Dulcimers,* 20
Smithsonian Folkways Recordings, 10
Smithsonian Institution, x, xi, 16
St. Clair, Arthur, 103
Sweet Songster, The, 63
Swick, Lilly McGhee Ward, 58, 60–61, 158n

Thomas, Jean: *The Singin' Gatherin',* 111
Thompson, Stith, 136
Turner, Anna Woods, 103–4
Tyler, Arthur D., and the Tyler dulcimer, 129–31, 165n

Underground Railroad, 22, 118
Utley, Francis, 8
Utter, Alma, 132
Utter, William T., 36, 103, 132, 165–66n

Vincent, Jenny Wells, 114, 115, 164n

Ward, Joseph, 97–98
Ward, Ken, 59–61, 158n
Ward, Kendra, 62
Weinrich, Bessie, 65, 133–40, 166–67n
Weinrich, Philip, 134
Wemmer, Faye, xi, *68,* 84, 141–44, 167n
White, Bird O. and Anne, 145–46, 167n
White, Bob, 58–59, 158n
Wilson, Anne Rayner, 147–49, 167n
Wilson, Frazer E., 102–104
Wood, Okey, and the Okey Wood dulcimer, 150–51, 167–68n
WOSU radio, 4, 95
Wright, Bertha Basham, 27–30, 155–56n
Wright, John, 60

Yost, Fielding "Frank," 124–25

Zimmerman, Mary, 128

Title Index

Page numbers in italic type indicate song lyrics and/or notation. The letter *n* following a page number indicates an Editors' Note. For titles included on the CD, see page 153.